The Jesus Conversation with Indians

The Jesus Conversation with Indians

Strategies and Methods for Introducing Jesus to First- and Second- Generation Indian Immigrants in America

Anush A. John, D.Min, MD

A Ministry Focus Paper Submitted To The Faculty Of The School Of Theology, Fuller Theological Seminary, In Partial Fulfillment Of The Requirements For The Degree Doctor of Ministry, October 2010

Cover Photo Credit: Susie Mey Photography

ISBN: 0692544127
ISBN 13: 9780692544129

Contents

Glossary[1]

Adharmasya. Irreligion.

Advaita philosophy. That branch of Hindu philosophy expounded by Sankara and that deals with the concept that the Atman and Brahman are essentially one.

Aham brahma asmi. "I am that" - the realization that the Atman is one with the Brahman

Ahimsa. The teaching of non-violence (non-injury).

Artharthin. A worshipper that desires wealth

Ashram. Retreat center, monastery

Atman. The essence of a person – the Self

Avatar. Incarnation of deity in human form. There are believed to be ten avatars.

Avta. A penitent worshipper

Bhagavadgita. The part of the epic Mahabharata which is the most favorite book of millions of Hindus. This book describes the way of devotion. (*Bhakti Marga*)

Bhakta. Devotee of God. (usually of the *Bhakti Marga*)

Bhakti. Devotion.

Bhakti Marga. Way of devotion.

Brahman. The Absolute Reality; God.

Brahmin. Also called Brahman, the group at the epitome of the social ladder, the priests.

Dasyus. The class of people below the four classes.

Devas. Divine beings

Dharma. Righteous way of living as enjoined by the sacred scriptures; virtue

Dharmasya. Religion.

Guru. Teacher

Jijnasu. A worshipper that seeks wisdom

Jnana Marga. Way of knowledge.

Jnanin. A worshipper who is a person of vision.

Kalki. The destroyer of darkness. He is the tenth avatar of Vishnu and will appear at the end of the current age.

Kshatriya. The warrior class.

Karma. Actions operating through the law of cause and effect.

Karma Marga. Way of action.

Krishna. One of the most popular incarnations (avatars) of Vishnu. He is the hero of the epic Mahabharata of which the Bhagavad Gita is a part.

Marga. Way.

Moskha. Liberation (usually, from the cycle of rebirth).

Nirguna. Personal devotion offered to an impersonal god that has no attributes. (contrasted with saguna)

Niyamas. The five-step mental requirements in the preparatory stage in the formal eight-stage yoga. Used in *Jnana Marga*.

Oriental-referring to the East or people from the East (compared to occidental – referring to the West or people from the West.

Puja (Pooja). Ritualistic sacrifices. The puja room was a small room in the house that was used for daily rituals. It often had pictures and idols of the specific god that the family worshipped.

Rajas. One who seeks god for power and fame

Ramayana. A narrative of Rama. One of two Hindu epics.

Saguna. Personal devotion offered to a personal god with attributes (contrasted with nirguna)

Samsara. The process of worldly life.

Samskara. Life-cycle ritual. There were usually sixteen rituals.

Satguru. Enlightened master.

Satvika. performance of disinterested action for action's sake

Siva (Shiva). One of the two main deities.

Sudra. The menial workers. They are the lowest of the four classes.

Tamas. loving god for fulfillment of carnal desires.

Upanishad. Secret teaching. There are 13 Upanishads, which are counted as scripture and are the foundational scripture for *Jnana Marga* – the way of knowledge.

Vaishya. The merchant class of the four classes.

Varnas. Color. The four classes are based on color differences.

Vedas. The oldest Hindu scriptures. There are four Vedas – the Rig veda, the yajur veda, the atharva veda and sama veda.

Vishnu. One of the two favorite gods worshipped in *Bhakti Marga*. The other one is Siva.

Yamas. Five ethical virtues in the preparatory stage in the formal eight-stage yoga. Used in *Jnana Marga*.

Yogi. One who practices yoga.

Notes:

1 Swami Sivananda, *The Divine Life Society*, http://www.dlshq.org/glossary.htm (accessed May 8, 2010).

Introduction

India is a land of a billion people. Every sixth person in the world is an Indian. Just on the basis of sheer numbers, it is reasonable to imagine that Indians would be found in many places of the world. According to a colonial diary from 1790, the first Indian who visited the United States was a man from Madras who came to Salem, Massachusetts, for a trade between the two countries.[2] In the past four and a half decades, the Indian population in America has increased from 5000 in 1960 to 2.3 million in 2005.[3] Between 2004 and 2005, the number of immigrants from India has increased by 20.7% (14,530). The number of new legal, permanent U.S. residents annually from India is second only to the number from Mexico.[4]

India, a socio-religiously diverse and complex sub-continent, embodies various cultures and religious traditions. Contemporary American society also exhibits an amalgamation of the indigenous culture and the various immigrant cultures that have migrated to its shores over the past four hundred years. When these two huge diverse cultures attempt to merge together, homogeneity is unlikely. The people caught in the middle of this merger are the second generation Indians in America.

There are mainly three[5] classes of Indians in America. The first generation Indian is that Indian who migrated from India to America. These people came to America predominantly to work and make money. These people are the Enterans[6] – since they entered the country from a different one. The Indian culture runs deep within the fabric of their lives, and so most of them maintain their cultural and religious exclusivism and identity, even in America's predominantly Christian culture.

The next group is the second generation Indian. This generation is more American in their outlook and mannerisms. However, they still have strong Indian ties because of their parents and the structure of the Indian family. As a result, they struggle to maintain their identity as they try to balance being an Indian at home and an American outside. The result is usually a vacillating nature - willing to be inclusive in certain cultural habits but exclusive in others. They are willing to adopt American cultural practices but tend to maintain their Indian religious identity. They are the Indian-Americans or Indericans. They are not fully Indians, nor are the fully Americans, but a strange amalgamation that combines both natures to form a peculiar culture of their own.

The Enteran and the Inderican are two extremes of the types of Indians in America. A third category of Indians includes everyone between the extremes of the Enteran and the Inderican. This group exists because of variations in specific family cultures, age, city of origin in India, socioeconomic status, and education, among others. The characteristics of the third group are unpredictable and fall anywhere between the continuum of the Enteran-Inderican axis. This explains the reason for the dissemination of this group. For example, a twenty-five-year-old first generation Indian from a "westernized" city in India will be more Inderican in nature than a second generation Indian born in an ultraconservative family in America. Indeed, the two main classes of Indians in America – Enterans and Indericans are merely broad generalizations. These categories assume that some merger takes place when two cultures meet. The difference is in the extent of that merger and its manifestation thereof.

However, it is possible that there may be a certain percentage of people who fall outside these categories. There may be the Inderican who is so American in culture that he or she has absolutely no ties to Indian culture. And there may the Enteran who is so Indian in culture that he or she is completely uninfluenced by American culture. These are, however, more theoretical than reality. The latter is more likely to be true than the former. That is, it is more possible to think of an Enteran who is totally uninfluenced by

American culture than of an Inderican who is totally uninfluenced by Indian culture. The reason for this is the almost fanatic bond that exists between the Indian and Indianness. It is extremely difficult to rid an Indian of his/her Indianness. Dilution of Indian culture can probably be seen after a few generations of mixed marriages or a few generations away from India, but, in the Enteran and the Inderican, the Indian ties are still strong. In addition, among the Indian immigrants, various major world religions are represented. The majority of them follow the Hindu way of life while others follow the Christian, Muslim, Jain, Buddhist, and Sikh traditions.

In such a socio-religious milieu, it has been extremely difficult for the American Christian culture to make a very strong spiritual impact on Enterans and Indericans. This is also true as far as spirituality and religion are concerned. The same reason for which Indian culture is hard to break into explains why Indian religion is hard to break into. This presents a challenge for anyone involved in Christian ministry among Indians. This study attempts to present strategies for effective evangelism among first- and second- generation Hindu diaspora in America, building on current theories of evangelism in multi-religious contexts. Two strategies are required for those at the two ends of the Enteran-Inderican axis. Modifications in strategy can be made for all those who are scattered between the two extremes, that is, the third group of Indians in America.

This book is limited in that a strategy to reach every Indian in America cannot be formulated. This is because of the complexity and interplay of five major non-Christian Indian religions – Hinduism, Buddhism, Jainism, Islam, and Sikhism – twenty-two major languages, educational and socio-economic disparity, the difference in immigration status, and the differences in belief of Hindus in their numerous gods. Thus, the study is limited to Hindus in general at the two ends of the first and second immigrant generation spectrum.

The first part of this book will look at the two generations of Indian cultures – that of the first generation and that of the second generation.[7] The first generation tends to maintain most of their socio-religious traditions - culturally and religiously. The second generation has a unique culture – one that is partly Indian and partly American. The first generation usually holds strong religious beliefs, having been raised in India. The second generation holds mixed beliefs and is more open to the postmodern tolerance of all religions. The American Church has had a decreased spiritual influence on both the first and second generation in varying degrees. This section will analyze the reasons for this lack of influence. Although there are several major world religions in India, Hinduism will be the focus of the discussion since it is the predominant Indian religion. In all other aspects of the discussion, generalizations will be made of Indian culture.

The second part of this book will look at the biblical and theological foundations of evangelism. Core biblical topics and post-modernism and their relevance to both the first and second generation Indians in the postmodern era will be discussed. The Hindu concept of *Bhakti* will also be looked at.[8] These topics, though diverse, have evangelism as the common thread that runs through them. Each topic will therefore be studied as related to evangelism.

In the third section, the understanding of the two Indian cultures and the theological foundations of evangelism will be used to develop strategies to introduce Jesus among first and second generation Indian Hindus in America. This work is for anyone who is involved in ministering to Indians in America, whether in Indian churches or other churches that minister to Indians.

Notes:

2 Arthur W. Helweg and Usha M. Helweg, *An Immigrant Success Story: East Indians in America* (Philadelphia: University of Pennsylvania Press, 1990), 45.
3 US Census Bureau, American Factfinder, United States General Demographic Characteristics: 2005, "Race," http://factfinder.census.gov/servlet/ADPTable?_bm=y&-geo_id=01000US&-ds_name=ACS_2005_EST_G00_&-_lang=en&-_caller=geoselect&-format= (accessed April 13, 2007).
4 Julia Gelatt and Deborah Meyers, "Legal Immigration to the United States Increased Substantially in FY 2005," Migration Policy Institute, October 2006, "Immigration Facts," no. 13 http://www.migrationpolicy.org/pubs/FS13_immigration_US_2006.pdf (accessed April 13, 2007).
5 Of course, there are many classes of Indians in America including those who are third- and fourth-generation immigrants, those who have intermarried with non-Indians, and those who moved to America from countries other than India. However, this work is focused on first generation Hindus who have migrated directly from India and second generation Hindus who are born to Indian parents.

6   "Enteran" refers to the first generation Indian immigrant who entered America. "Inderican" refers to the second generation Indian in America, who is an Indian American. The term "Indian" is used to refer to both groups together and to those people who are of Indian origin in general – the context will clarify the difference.

7   The first-generation Indians are those Indians that migrated to America from India while the second-generation Indians are those that were born in America to Indian parents.

8   This book intends to build on the centrality of understanding the concept of "*Bhakti*" in Hinduism. The relationship between *Bhakti*, Hinduism, and its relevance in evangelism will be used in forming the strategies for evangelism.

Part One

Cultural and Religious Background

One

Enterans - The First Generation - "Vikram Patel"

The Enteran in America is the closest representation of an Indian in America in every aspect - social, religious, and cultural. In successive generations from the Enteran onward, the Indianness of an Indian in America, according to the Second Law of Thermodynamics, constantly reduces in nature. The Enteran in America is almost like a fish out of water – transplanted from a milieu he or she is comfortable in to a completely different one. Surprisingly, the Enteran does not develop pronounced amphibian features in the new setting and yet survives. This chapter presents an overview of the Enterans including their social, economic, and religious makeup, in addition to key features of Indian culture as relevant to evangelism and their immigration to America, their adaptation to the new environment, and their success in America.

SALIENT FEATURES OF INDIAN CULTURE
Since it has been several millennia since Hinduism has been in existence in India, many of the features of Indian culture are synonymous with Hindu culture. Some of the basic underlying features are its democratic nature, tolerance, its caste system, superstitions, and the nature of family.

DEMOCRATIC NATURE AND TOLERANCE
There is a great variety of individual cultures that make up the Indian culture. The number of gods in Hinduism totals a staggering thirty-three million.

Language, food habits, and customs differ in general from state to state. It is a country with diverse cultures: three major race groups, four prominent religious communities, and sixteen language categories including English. Although India's unity has been challenged, the country has survived as the world's most populous democracy.[9] The fact that India still remains as one country in spite of its internal differences is testament to its democratic nature.

Tolerance toward other views, beliefs, and opinions is characteristic of Indian culture. Since India was isolated from the rest of the world by the vast expanse of water on the east, south, and west and by the mighty Himalayas to the north, Hinduism was thus shielded from major changes that happened in the rest of the world. The few conquerors that managed to break through the mountains could control only small portions of northern India. These invaders soon settled down in India and came to terms with the brahmans, and Indians accepted them as a part of themselves. This reflects the essence of Hinduism – Hinduism accepts everyone and every belief and every culture as a part of its own.[10]

CASTE SYSTEM

One of the banes of India has been the classification of people and predetermination of profession based on birth. The caste system was born on the basis of color differences between the darker Dravidians (the original inhabitants of India) and lighter Aryans (European invaders). The earliest indication of class ranking was seen in Rigveda 10.90.[11] This creation hymn tells of the sacrifice of a giant Purusa, a cosmic man with a thousand eyes and feet. From his limbs and organs all the prominent features of the world were formed, including the social classes (*varnas*) from his body. The brahman – the priests - was his mouth; his two arms became the *kshatriya* – the warriors; his thighs became the merchant class - the *vaishya*; and his feet produced the *sudra* – menial workers. This is a dramatic change in the order of importance of professions. In Aryan societies of the Middle East and Europe, the warrior class always occupied the highest level of leadership, but in India the priestly class occupies the highest tier of respect. Thus there are four social divisions based on occupation.

Another Hindu scripture, the Manusmriti, written between 200 B.C. and A.D. 200, added another class of people who had no place among the four *varnas*. (Manusmriti 10.45 ff.) He placed them below the class of *sudras* and called them *dasyus*. These are impure groups whose hereditary work is that of hunters, fishermen, leather workers, executioners, and handlers of corpses. They are unclean and must live outside the villages. Hindus are not permitted to associate with them or teach them the scriptures.[12]

SUPERSTITIONS

Indians hold many superstitions.[13] This is related to the law of *karma*, the belief in cause and effect of all things. Everything is caused by something, and everything results in something else. It is difficult for an Indian to believe that anything can happen by pure chance. That is the basis of the belief in innumerable superstitions. Many omens relate to animals, birds, and reptiles. The most auspicious omen is to see an elephant when one is on a journey, for it represents Ganesha, the god of good luck and the remover of obstacles. The cawing of a crow in one's house foretells the coming of guests. A peacock seen while on a journey is said to be good, but hearing its shrill call indicates robbery by highwaymen. A dog howling near a sick man's chamber predicts his death. Seeing a cat or a cow's face early in the morning brings ill luck. A sparrow is encouraged to build a nest in a new house for good fortune. The wall lizard boasts the most superstitions. Every movement of this reptile holds some significance; indeed, a science called the Gowli Shastra enumerates these. The color, spots, stripes, chirping, or twittering of the lizard and where it falls on a person's body are said to indicate future happenings. Leaving on a journey is a very important occasion, and precautions have to be taken depending on the importance of the journey. There are several beliefs linked with starting on a journey. A sneeze or terms of dissuasion like "Stay, don't go," or "Where are you going?" used accidentally by someone at this crucial time are ill omens and a person must start again if this happens. It is considered auspicious to see cow dung, cereals, paddy, cotton, hay, or a newlywed before starting on a journey. There is also a strong belief in the power of dreams, as divine warnings. Dreaming of gods, demons, auspicious animals, or any other auspicious thing is good. Whereas, dreaming of gold or iron, falling stars, or earthquakes is bad.

Daily life is governed by do's and don'ts for each day of the week. Thus, Monday is not an auspicious day for shaving or Tuesday for washing one's hair or Saturday for buying oil. Most of these superstitions are linked to the respective planets presiding over each day (according to the Hindu calendar). The kitchen is virtually the temple of a Hindu home and the highest levels of hygiene are expected to be maintained. Most Hindus do not enter a kitchen with their shoes on, as it is said to induce the wrath of the gods. Another belief linked to this was that before eating their food, people sprinkled water around their plates supposedly in remembrance of their ancestors.

Some other popular superstitions are, if a person hiccups, it is believed that someone is talking about him or remembering him. The falling of utensils on the floor foretells the coming of guests. These are just a few of the examples. There are innumerable superstitions which dictate the day to day living of millions of Indians.[14]

FAMILY

Families in most parts of India are of the patriarchal type. The father is the head of the house, and his decisions are usually unchallenged by the rest of the family. The mother has a highly respected position in the family. The word *"patni"* or wife means the person who sits next to her husband at the time of worship.[15] Once children are born, the lives of the parents revolve around them.

Children are expected to stay with parents until they are married and are ready to take care of themselves independently. There is not a lot of mobility in India. Thus children stay in the same city or village as their parents and, over many years, one finds that everyone in a village is indirectly related to each other. Large joint families still exist today where all the siblings and their families stay together in the same house.

SOCIAL AND ECONOMIC BACKGROUND

The most recent wave of immigration to date occurred in the late 1990s and early 2000 during the Internet boom. Indians are well represented, especially in academia, information technology, and medicine. There were over four thousand professors of Indian origin and thirty-three thousand Indian-born students in American universities in 1997-1998. The American Association of Physicians of Indian Origin lists a membership of thirty-five thousand. In 2000, Fortune magazine estimated the wealth generated by Indian Silicon Valley entrepreneurs at around $250 billion. Though the Indian diaspora in the US is largely concentrated in metropolitan areas such as Philadelphia, Atlanta, Chicago, Dallas, Los Angeles, New York, San Francisco, Detroit, and Houston, almost every state in the US has a community of Indians.[16]

Sodowsky and Carey did a study on Asian Indians who live in the western part of Texas. They had a sample population of ninety-six Asian Indians who responded to the survey: 73 percent of them had graduate degrees, 13 percent of them had undergraduate degrees, and 13 percent of them had completed high school and some college. Their study further showed that 62 percent of their sample population were professionals and 31 percent were university students.[17] "Although (India) is the second most populous country in the world, it has made considerable advancements in food production, industrialization, and general economic development. It contains a large contingent of intellectual people and is one of the largest exporters of highly educated talent in the world."[18] "Few modern Americans are surprised to find that their dentist or lawyer is of Indian origin, or are shocked to hear how vital Indians have been to California's high-tech industry. In ways big and small, Indians are changing the world."[19]

HIERARCHY AND KARMA

India's social structure and relations have been essentially unchanged for two millennia. This structure has been accepted by Hindu society through inheritance. The caste system plays a tremendous role in the Indian family. Who you are and whom you will marry are determined by the caste system. In addition, within the family, one's position, and, therefore, the respect that accompanies it, is affected by the birth order since Indians respect those older than themselves.[20] With the Enterans, the lines of separation between the classes are very hazy in most matters related to day-to-day living. However, the caste system still matters in important issues like marriage and death.

Each person, according to Hindu belief, is a product of what happened in the past and a link to what will happen in the future. Thus, there is a general feeling of resignation to one's fate and to the predetermination of one's current position. In contrast, a Western individual's success and failure are attributed to the individual's own capacities and not to one's actions in the past, and so failure in American society is considered a deficiency of the individual and not of the hand he was dealt.[21]

FAMILY VS. INDIVIDUAL

In the traditional Indian family, the family is more important than each individual. Fenton surveyed Asian Indians in Atlanta to determine what they valued most. Family was their favorite and it ranked higher than religions and "Indian character, arts and language."[22] Thus, individuals are not permitted to do anything that will tarnish the family honor, and the goals of the individual will be subservient to the goals of the family. This is counter to the western mindset. Here, the individual – his or her dreams, goals, ambitions, and desires – are preeminent, in spite of the family.[23] Most Indians feel a moral obligation and responsibility toward family members. Thus, parents take care of their children until they are married, including paying for as much of their education as they can afford. They will also care for them after marriage until the new family can stand on their own feet. Indian children, too, feel the obligation to care for their aging parents. Often children have their parents move in with them or stay very close to them so that they can be cared for. Many Enterans still have family in India, and it is not uncommon for them to make frequent visits to see the extended family.

Enterans tend to hold on to the family values they were raised with. Sharmila Rudrappa worked at a women's shelter in Chicago and gives an example of the difficulty Enterans have to shirk their Indian thinking. She talks of an Enteran woman abused by her husband. "She'd only been in the States for about a year. I had to explain to her that she's not in India anymore. She can do a lot more here than she can there. She could get a divorce. She could get a job. And she didn't have to listen to everything her family said now because they are so far away. But it's so hard to get her to stop thinking in those terms."[24]

SOCIAL SUCCESS AND COMMITMENT TO INDIAN CULTURE

Success in India is measured in terms of how well loved one is by his or her extended family. Thus, success is relationship based. Once the Enterans come to America, their views change. Success in America is defined materially. Thus, Enterans are more likely to show their success by their profession and possession of houses, expensive cars, and a lavish lifestyle.

Most Enterans continue to hold on to their cultural heritage and practices. They preserve their native language and food habits; they keep track of special Indian days of the year, contemporary events that are happening in India, and even sporting events. They are usually part of an Indian cultural organization, which helps them to actively celebrate their Indianness.[25]

OVERVIEW OF HINDUISM

The term "Hinduism" was introduced around 1830 by the British to refer principally to the culture and practices of the non-Islamic people of the Indian subcontinent. Hinduism literally means "the belief of the people of India." It is the predominant faith of India as 85 percent of Indians classify themselves as Hindus.

Hinduism arose among a people who had no significant contact with the biblical religions. Hindu teaching does not consist of alternative answers to the questions asked by western faiths.... The beliefs on which Hindus insist relate to problems that are especially acute in the Indian environment and the hopes of Hindus are shaped by what seems desirable and possible under the special conditions of Indian life.[26]

Hinduism does not have just one single authoritative religious testament but has been defined by many scriptural texts initially transmitted orally and later written in the Sanskrit language. It is impossible to define Hinduism because of the variety of its practice. There can be potentially millions of ways of being a practicing Hindu.[27]

Hinduism is more than just a religion. It is a way of life. There are three main classes of Hinduism based on the method used to attain liberation. The first and oldest one is *Karma Marga*.

KARMA MARGA - THE WAY OF ACTION

Karma Marga's main books are the *Vedas* and the *Laws of Manu*. Its primary ritualistic form is sacrifices, and its key concepts are karma and rebirth.

The concept of karma is an idea central to Hinduism and manifests itself in the daily lives of Hindus. The underlying belief is that one's fate is controlled by one's deeds. When combined with the doctrine of rebirth, it follows that one's fate in the next life or lives is determined by one's actions in the current one, just as one's circumstances in the current life have been determined by one's actions in the past life or lives. Fenton explains:

In its most rudimentary sense, karma means "an action." In ethical discussions it means an action that is morally important because it is an act required or prohibited by the codes of dharma. Karma means, next, the unseen energy believed to be generated by the performance of such a dutiful or undutiful act. Long after the visible act has been completed, this energy continues in existence. At an appropriate time, it discharges itself upon the doer causing that person to experience the consequences of the original act. Accumulated karma gives to some persons well-merited freedom from disease, sharp minds, good looks, virtuous dispositions, and long lives. It brings the opposite of these benefits to others for equally valid reasons. Karma is believed to exert itself with particular force at those times in our individual careers when we are about to be reborn into the world… At the moment of our conception in the womb, the moral force of our past deeds is believed to move us, with perfect justice, into a new family and a new cast.[28]

Thus our actions in the past determined our present, and those in the present determine our future.

JNANA MARGA - THE WAY OF KNOWLEDGE

Jnana Marga's main books are the *Upanishads*. Its primary ritualistic forms are meditation and yoga, and its key concepts are Moksha, Brahman, and Atman.

The understanding that knowledge gives power is common to many religious traditions. Hindus who follow the way of knowledge recognize that common knowledge is good only for temporal, worldly matters. It is insufficient for eternal, spiritual issues. Thus, they seek an exceptional kind of knowledge, a mystical knowledge of reality that would open the portals of the universe. In this quest for understanding the universe, the priests turned from the external sacrifices to the possible infinite spiritual connections of those sacrifices. They recognized that the liturgy associated with it was beyond mere words – it had powerful connections with the outer world, and they craved to understand that connection. Their focus was on the term *Brahman*, which was the sum and substance of vedic literature. They reasoned that, if the simple term *Brahman* held so much power, why would the knowledge of Brahman not open the doors of supreme mystical knowledge? Thus, the focus was moved from the rituals to the priests performing the rituals. Indeed, the rituals were now seen as inadequate to relate with immortality. Knowledge, on the other hand, was infinite and could be acquired with discipline. As a result, the practice of sacrifice declined, and the practice of meditation increased. Rejection of rituals to pursue meditation was the basis of the way of knowledge and came into full expression in compositions called the *Upanishads*, which are the fundamental scriptures of the way of knowledge.

The word "Upanishad" means a secret teaching. The *Upanishads* are "secrets" in that they tell of realities not superficially apparent and express truths intended to be studied only by inquirers of special fitness. The authors of the *Upanishads* acknowledge the usefulness of the priests' sacrifices, but they deny the ultimate worth of these sacrifices. They were concerned with the concept of death in the light of karma, rebirth and caste. They felt trapped in an endless world of lives and deaths. The Way of Action no longer offered them happiness, even in heaven. Their great desire was liberation from the bonds of karma. They did not want more lives. Rather, they wanted freedom in an unchanging existence in a different nature, free from all necessity of death and birth.[29]

To the eternal question – "What is the Universe?" - the authors of the *Upanishads* offered some insights regarding the Brahman. First, it is spirit; that is, it is not a material thing. The second insight is that Brahman is not a dead thing, but the source of the world and all its life. The authors could not find words to describe Brahman because it is indescribable. Since it cannot be seen or felt or sensed in any way, Brahman is beyond the power of all verbal description. Thus it is impossible to know Brahman itself. Thus, in their search for the source of the universe, the authors of the *Upanishads* discovered an immaterial, life-giving Oneness that is beyond description.[30]

To the next biggest question that man asks, "Who am I?" the sages of the *Upanishads* similarly answer more negatively than positively. The real person, they say, is not the body, the mind, the intellect, or the psyche as a whole; and it is not perceptible through the senses or known in ordinary states of consciousness. The authors of the *Upanishads* affirm that Atman is the root from which a person is reborn time after time.

Atman is the stuff of consciousness. ... (It) conveys at least the idea of something that is not material. The soul within us cannot be tasted, heard, or smelled as material objects can. It cannot be weighed or dissected; yet its reality is undeniable because the reality of atman is attested by the fact of our possessing consciousness. Whereas a Westerner might argue, "I think, therefore I am," a Hindu would say, "I am conscious, therefore I am."[31]

Thus, the answers to the questions – "What is the universe?" and "Who am I?" are funneled to one answer – a nonmaterial presence. As the sages pondered these questions, they received the epiphany that the real universe and the real self - both with similar qualities - were identical in essence. This knowledge quelled the hopelessness of the concept of endless births and decaying deaths. Since the real self of every person was actually one with the Brahman, death did not matter anymore; neither did divisions like the caste system. Individual identity did not matter anymore. Salvation, then, was in entering the peace of being one with the Brahman. Sankara[32] postulated that ignorance of this knowledge is, therefore, the impediment to salvation. Thus, one's desire should be to dispel this ignorance of one's actual identity. One can hope to attain liberation if the devotee is willing to renounce attachment to the world and its desire and seek salvation through the way of knowledge. Since it is not easy to renounce desires and worldly attachment, the zealous devotee has to adopt certain extreme measures, like the practice to perfect oneself in five ethical virtues (*yamas*) and the five-step mental requirements (*niyamas*) in the formal eight-stage yoga or discipline of the way of knowledge. To complete the eight stages, the devotees are encouraged to forsake normal life and seek solitude, usually in the mountains or forests.[33] The goal of meditation and yoga is to receive the full knowledge that the Brahman and Atman are one and to experience that oneness with the Brahman.

BHAKTI MARGA - THE WAY OF DEVOTION

Bhakti Marga's major scripture is the *Bhagavad Gita*. Its primary ritualistic action is devotional worship, and its key concept is *Bhakti*.

The *Bhakti Marga* places its hope for liberation in the power of a personal God of the universe. This *marga* is most similar to western faiths. This shift in Hindu thinking is a major one from impersonal principles like *karma* and *dharma* in the vedic tradition to belief in a personal God that accepts devotion. The term *Bhakti* implies the unreserved loyalty and willingness to serve, combined with gratitude and trust. The two most popular theistic movements in Hinduism are centered on Siva and on Vishnu. The worshipers of Siva are known as Saivas, and the worshipers of Visnu, as Vaisnavas.[34]

Worship of Siva

Unlike the *advaita* philosophy in *Jnana Marga* where the worshipper loses his identity in becoming one with God, this union with God in worship produces a feeling of personal intimacy. After the intimate experience, devotees are expected to live in joy and freedom. Indeed, in the *advaita* doctrine, it is thought of as being blasphemous for human beings to identify themselves with God.

Adherents of this branch are seen mainly in the south Indian state of Tamil Nadu. A certain number of Hindus worship what they say is the female counterpart of Siva called Durga.[35]

Worship of Visnu:

Fenton describes Visnu:

The Visnu of the Vedas is associated with the sun and is seen as promoting growth. He is present in plants and trees, provides food, and protects unborn babies in the womb. He rides a sun-eagle, wears a sun like jewel on his breast, and is armed with a discus that is clearly the orb of the sun. But he is not the sun, and thus his jurisdiction is not limited to a single part of the natural world.[36]

The *Bhagavad Gita*, a work of the second or first century BC, is the classical scripture expounding the way of devotion. When it was written, it was so well accepted that it was incorporated immediately into the Mahabharata. Even though the author reluctantly accepts that all forms of Hinduism can lead to salvation, he overrules the view of an impersonal Brahman for a personal Lord and objects to the need for renunciation, claiming instead that one can attain salvation without interfering with regular life.[37]

Perhaps the most important of Vaisnava thought is the concept of incarnation. Hindus recognize ten such avatars or human manifestations of Visnu.[38] Kalki, the tenth avatar, is yet to come. He is a rider on a winged white horse and is believed to appear at the conclusion of the current age to destroy the wicked. Of these ten avatars, Rama and Krsna are now the most popular of all Hindu divinities.

Regarding the worship of Krsna, in addition to the usual worship of Krsna, another scripture called the *Harivamsa Purana*, written about AD 300, claimed additional information and stories about Krsna, the seventh avatar of Visnu, especially about his early years. Based on this information, sects of worshipers of the child Krsna were founded. The Hare Krsna movement, born from this, is popular in the West.

In terms of the worship of Rama, Rama's story was first written by Valmiki in about the fourth century BC in the epic Ramayana, and the tradition may be based on an actual person. The relation between the cults of Rama and Krsna is cordial and is possible since both of them are avatars of Visnu. In Vaisnava communities today, there are celebrations and festivals for both deities together.[39]

RELIGIOUS BACKGROUND

Fenton estimates that, of the 800,000 people of Indian origin in the country in 1985, 65 percent probably came from a Hindu background.[40] It would be natural to assume that immigrants would eventually syncretize their beliefs with the majority religion of the adoptive country, but that is not found to be true. Herberg wrote:

Of the immigrant who came to this country it was expected that, sooner or later, either in his own person or through his children, he would give up virtually everything he had brought with him from the "old country"-his language, his nationality, his manner of life-and would adopt the ways of his new home. Within broad limits, however, his becoming an American did not involve his abandoning the old religion in favor of some native American substitute. Quite the contrary, not only was he expected to retain his old religion, as he was not expected to retain his old language or nationality, but such was the shape of America that it was largely in and through his religion that he, or rather his children and grandchildren, found an identifiable place in American life.[41]

In fact, the opposite was found to be true – immigrants became more religious than they were in India.

Immigrants are religious - by all counts more religious than they were before they left home - because religion is one of the important identity markers that helps them preserve individual self-awareness and cohesion in a group.... In the United States, religion is the social category with clearest meaning and acceptance in the host society, so the emphasis on religious affiliation and identity is one of the strategies that allow the immigrant to maintain self-identity while simultaneously acquiring community acceptance. That makes religion one of the most powerful of the value systems...[42]

The reasons for this increase in religious interest are "loneliness, the romanticizing of memories, the guilt for imagined desertion of parents and other relatives, and the search for community and identity in a world of strangers."[43] Religion becomes less taken for granted under the auspices of a secular United States, and that forces worshippers to define their beliefs.[44]

The challenge that most new immigrants in the United States face is how to be able to "fit in'" but at the same time maintain one's identity and integrity.

Hindu Enterans achieve this by using Hinduism and by maintaining their religious beliefs, which they brought with them into the country. Though it may seem that becoming an American and staying as a Hindu are contrary to each other, the Enterans have solved the dilemma by developing a Hindu American community and identity. Thus, religion has become the key symbol of identity and of difference from American society and has come to represent their Indian heritage, so that being an Indian means to be a Hindu.[45]

The Indian tradition has been not to confront or convert those who disagree with their views, but to absorb by toleration and acceptance. Hinduism in India adapted itself to challenges over the millennia posed by Jainism, Buddhism, Islamic invaders, and, most recently, Western colonial missionaries by incorporating certain elements of their traditions into their own.[46] Similarly, Hinduism has adapted and conformed to the new American cultural context forming an American Hinduism.

Some strategies of adaptation include unity, small groups, and cultural organizations. Unity posits a united Hinduism seen in America.

An ecumenical Hinduism is developing in the United States that unites deities, rituals, sacred texts, and people in temples and programs in ways that would not be found together in India….Emphasis is placed upon an all-India Hindu "great tradition," on devotion to major deities, and upon some elements of the Sanskrit tradition…. Study and devotional groups use universally accepted Hindu texts, such as the *Bhagavad-Gita* and the *Ramayana*. Languages used are Sanskrit for rituals and English for instruction, commentary and business.[47]

Small groups are another means of adapting. Indian immigrants coming to the United States from their "little traditions" are here socialized into a pan-Indian Hinduism.

One of the characteristics of diasporic Hinduism seems to be the … tendency to develop groups for study and worship. Many Hindu immigrants may never join such groups. Still there has been a radical proliferation of such religious associations. The 1995 directory of the Federation of Hindu Associations lists over thirty associations for southern California alone.[48]

An important method by which Indian immigrants maintain their cohe-siveness is through Hindu/Indian cultural organizations. Religion has al-ways been one of the most powerful reasons for group formation. Two such groups – Satsang groups and Bala Vihars – have proliferated among the im-migrant Indian community in the United States. Both Satsangs and Bala Vihars are forms of religious practice that do not typically exist in India. In fact, group religious activity does not exist in traditional Hinduism. In India, Hindus worship largely as families or as individuals, in their homes or a temple. Larger groups at the temple may be present to witness the *pooja*[49] performed by the priest on behalf of the community. Only festivals are cel-ebrated communally by a village. These two organizations represent two dif-ferent strategies adopted by Indian immigrants to re-create a Hindu Indian environment on foreign soil. The first, which largely targets adults, celebrates and reenacts religious practice. The second is directed at teaching the children about the religion. Both the structure and the culture of these groups help its participants to compete more advantageously with members of other groups. As such, it is not surprising that the latest wave of immigrants have formed ethnoreligious organizations in their attempt to adapt to American society.[50]

THE MOVE TO AMERICA

Emigration from India has been a dominant behavioral pattern on the sub-continent for centuries. From the time of the Indus Valley civilization in 2600 BC, whose merchants frequented other lands, to the sixth to eleventh cen-turies AD when Indians developed trade networks with Southeast Asia to trade with Africa during the British rule in the twentieth century, Indians have constantly been on the move. The nineteenth century brought a radical change to the character of India's diaspora: small-scale emigration became a mass movement to provide cheap labor for Britain's colonies.[51] Since India's independence in 1947, emigration has continued, not only to England and the New Commonwealth, but also to the United States, Australia, and the Middle East. Large-scale movement to the United States began in the middle 1950s, especially among students. Revised immigration regulations in the 1960s em-phasized skill rather than race. Thus, educated Indians, especially from the

Indian states of Punjab, Gujarat, and Kerala, took advantage of these policy changes. As a result, the West gained a contingent of competent immigrants.[52]

The first Indian to visit the United States was a man from Madras in 1790. According to a colonial diary, he came to Salem, Massachusetts, for a trade between the two countries. Indian presence is reported at Salem's 1851 Fourth of July celebration, also in the California gold rush of 1849, and at the Parliament of religions held at the Chicago World Columbian Exposition in 1853.[53] In 1910, there were ten thousand Indians in America. By 1960, that number increased to 17,000. However, in the next ten years, the number of Indians in the United States population jumped to 75,000.[54] The United States census of 1990 showed an Indian population of 815,447, and, by 2000, that number had doubled to 1,678,765.[55]

It is generally agreed that there were two waves of Indian immigrants to America in the last half century. Most of the first wave of immigrants came under the "special skills" provision of the 1965 immigration act, and thus were highly educated people who entered professional or managerial careers. Once here, however, they sponsored the immigration of relatives under the family reunification aspect of the 1965 act,[56] and thus the second wave of immigrants, coming since the early 1980s, often do not have the same educational or professional status as the first group of immigrants.

The year 1965 was decisive for immigration into the United States. The passage of Public Law 89-236 (effective 1968) amended America's immigration rules. The old national-origins system was abolished, and the quota system was revised so that Asians and Africans gained equal status with Europeans for immigration. This set off a new wave of immigration to the United States, with a massive influx of highly talented individuals from Asia, Africa, and South America. They often arrived at New York's Kennedy Airport. Those who had contacts lived with them, but those who did not settled in Flushing and Queens. Soon they moved out to more affluent areas of New Jersey and Long Island. Within five years, East Indian radio programs were broadcast, newspapers were founded, and Asian Indian associations and temple societies were formed.[57]

In the 1990s, California replaced New York as the center for Enterans, mainly because "Silicon Valley" became the center of computers and high technology. Enterans migrated to places of greater job opportunity.

The social experiences of the two groups or waves of immigrants were different, too. The first-wave immigrants came mainly for economic reasons and intended to stay only as long as they needed to. They were focused on their careers and in their objective of making as much money as possible so that they could return to India. Their social lives were minimal, mainly with the few other Indians around them. However, as time went on, their children became older, and it became less and less likely that they would return to India.[58] It then became important for them to interact with other Indians around them. The second wave of immigrants, on the other hand, came to an already established social structure.[59]

WHY ENTERANS CAME TO AMERICA

There are several reasons why Enterans come to America. Six of them are given here.[60] First is *economic* reasons. Well-employed professionals of the upper-middle class of Indian society are willing to disrupt the lives of their family to start an uncertain life anew in the West because of money. They see America as providing unlimited and easily accessible wealth. They intend to return within a few years after accumulating a sufficient amount of money.

The second reason is *employment*. India's industrial and technological development has led to the formation of the largest middle class in Asia; its strong emphasis on education has made it the third largest supplier of scientists in the world, behind only the United States and the Soviet Union. Ironically, the demand was unable to keep up with the supply, and thus many of these highly educated and technically qualified professionals have emigrated to the West, Africa, other parts of Asia, and the Middle East. In the late 1960s, there was a shortage of doctors and engineers in the United States because of the Vietnam War. Recruiters from the United States went to various parts of the Third World, recruiting skilled labor. Indians arrived to take the available jobs, thinking to stay for a few years. "And so we arrived thinking we were embarking on an adventure … thinking we'd stay for only maybe two years. But the two years have now become thirty, and we're still here."[61] Emigrants to the United States primarily originate from three Indian states: Gujarat – about 60 percent, Punjab – about 35 percent, and Kerala contributing about 10 percent.[62]

The third reason is *education*. Large-scale movement of students to the United States began in the middle 1950s. The United States was perceived as being superior in technology, business, and general sciences.

The fourth reason is *family*. Many of the second wave immigrants in the 1980s came because their families were already here in America. Currently, since more of the initial Enterans prefer to continue living in America rather than returning to India as they had originally planned, their children marry people from India and bring their spouses back to America. Thus, there are many Indians who come to America having married Enterans or Indericans.

The fifth reason is *social opportunities*. Indians who struggle in India be-cause of existing social strictures can have a second chance in a foreign, un-biased country. For example, widows and divorcees will not have the same stigma they face in India.

The sixth reason is that emigration is *prestigious*. Though outlooks are significantly changing now, emigration to America is seen as more prestigious and comfortable than living in India. For any of the above reasons, Enterans have migrated and continue to migrate to the United States.

PROBLEMS OF EMIGRATION

When the Enterans arrived on the shores of America, they realized that all was not as perfect as they had visualized. They faced a host of problems related to the differences between the two cultures.

Indian immigrants left behind a family-oriented society to embrace a cul-ture, which is more individual oriented. To many Indians, coming to the United States was a lonesome experience.[63] Those Enterans who came in the first wave were in a way pioneers among the Indian community. They came to the United States as professionals hoping to stay for a few years and thus were separated from their families. Their mannerisms, accents, and culture were different and they felt alienated and quite out of place as a minority in a completely different setting than the one they were used to.

These new immigrants may experience acculturation stress and nostalgia for their native country. In the dominant society of their adopted country they may encounter oppressive socio-political experiences, and reciprocally, they may distance themselves from the dominant group. They may also try to maintain distinctiveness of their national identity and cultural attitudes relative to that of other ethnic and minority groups. Hence, first generation Asian/Indian immigrants probably experience isolation and neglect when they venture outside of the tight socially supportive community of compatriots and kin in the United States from the old country.[64]

Enterans have homes in their home country, India, as well as in the host country, the United States. Instead of being bounded by loyalties to just one or the other, these individuals negotiate culture, family, and national communities both here and there. Thus, the majority of Enterans cannot be confined to the geographical and cultural boundaries of any one single nation-state, so they have divided loyalties.[65]

The economic situation that drew Enterans to America gradually began to change. For example, a cutback in the aerospace industry in 1970 resulted in many unemployed engineers. Gradually the ecstasy turned to bitterness as a result of these economic realities.

In spite of the obvious difficulties that Enterans faced, no one dared return and risk being thought of as a failure by friends and family. Since self-esteem is of great importance to family honor, an immigrant returning home without a fortune would have to suffer personal ridicule, and his entire family would be brought to shame. It was better, then, to hang on and suffer. Many also had faith that things would change for the better. Why did people keep coming? One major reason was that East Indians in America or on return trips to India kept up the stories of their mythical success. When they wrote home to India, they continued to tell stories of success, not of unemployment or low-status jobs. Indians continued to come to America in spite of the obvious difficulties. People who had sons or brothers in the United States continued to receive reports of such success, so the mentality in India was, "If his son can be successful in America, my son can also." Thus, those who had such contacts did not believe the official reports but relied on informal information.[66]

Notes:

9 Helweg, *An Immigrant Success Story,* 7.

10 John Y. Fenton, *Religions of Asia* (New York: St. Martin's Press, 1983), 37-38.

11 The Aryans wrote the Vedas during the period between 3500 and 1800 BC. The Rig Veda is the first of four vedas – the oldest of Hindu religious scripture, written between 1700-1100 B.C.

12 Fenton, *Religions of Asia,* 63.

13 A superstition is a system of beliefs or notions, not usually based on reason or knowledge, in or of the ominous significance of a particular thing, circumstance, or occurrence and the acts based on those beliefs.This definition is adapted from http://dictionary.reference.com/browse/superstition (accessed september 25, 2010).

14 Sikhnet, "Popular Indian Superstitions" http://www.sikhnet.com/sikhnet/discussion.nsf /By +Topic/9D4727920CFE8F7987256A340050CF72!OpenDocument (accessed March 2, 2008).

15 Kondoor Abraham, *The Asian Indian in the United States,* (Pompano Beach, FL: Desh Videsh Publishing, 2003), 6-7.

16 Wikipedia, "Non-resident Indian and Person of Indian Origin," http://en.wikipedia.org/wiki/Non-resident_Indian_and_Person_of_Indian_Origin#Indians_in_the_U.S. (accessed March 1, 2008).

17 Gargi Sodowsky and John Carey, "Relationships between Acculturation-Related Demographics and Cultural Attitudes of an Asian-Indian Immigrant Group," *Journal of Multicultural Counseling and Development* 16, no. 3 (July 1988): 117-136 Quoted in Abraham, *The Asian Indian in the United States,* 11.

18 Helweg, *An Immigrant Success Story,* 5-7.

19 Michael Elliot, "India Awakens," *Time Magazine,* June 18, 2006, 38.

20 Sathi Sengupta Dasgupta, *On the Trail of an Uncertain Dream: Indian Immigrant Experience in America* (New York: AMS Press, 1989), 66-70.

21 Ibid., 66-70.

22 John Y. Fenton, *Transplanting Religious Traditions: Asian Indians in America* (New York: Praeger, 1988), 201.

23 Dasgupta, *On the Trail of an Uncertain Dream,* 66-70.

24 Sharmila Rudrappa, *Ethnic Routes to Becoming American: Indian Immigrants and the Cultures of Citizenship* (Rutgers, NJ: Rutgers University Press, 2004), 173.

25 Dasgupta, *On the Trail of an Uncertain Dream,* 88-90.

26 Fenton, *Religions of Asia,* 37.

27 Rudrappa, *Ethnic Routes to Becoming American,* 120.

28 Fenton, *Religions of Asia,* 68.

29 Fenton, *Religions of Asia,* 79-82.

30 Fenton, *Religions of Asia,* 83.

31 Fenton, *Religions of Asia,* 85-86.

32 Thought to have lived in AD 788–820, he is credited with the exposition of this philosophy called the Advaita Vedanta.

33 Fenton, *Religions of Asia*, 86-91.

34 Fenton, *Religions of Asia*, 96-97.

35 Durga is worshiped mainly in Gujarat, Rajasthan, Bengal and regions of northeast India, including Nepal. Other names by which she is known are: Uma, Parvati, Candi, Bhairavi, Camunda, Kali. See Fenton, *Religions of Asia*, 101.

36 Fenton, *Religions of Asia*, 103.

37 Fenton, *Religions of Asia*, 105.

38 They are Matsya, Kurma, Varaha, Narasimha, Vamana, Parasurama, Krsna, Rama, Buddha, and Kalki.

39 Fenton, *Religions of Asia*, 112.

40 Fenton, *Transplanting Religious Traditions*, 28.

41 Will Herberg, *Protestant-Catholic-Jew: An Essay in American Religious Sociology* (New York: Oxford University Press, 1960), 27-28, Quoted by R. Stephen Warner, *Gatherings in Diaspora: Religious Communities and the New Immigration*, ed. R. Stephen Warner and Judith G. Wittner (Philadelphia: Temple University Press, 1998), 16.

42 Raymond Williams, *Religions of Immigrants from India and Pakistan: New Threads in the American Tapestry* (Cambridge: Cambridge University Press, 1988), 11-12.

43 Timothy Smith, "Religion and Ethnicity in America," *American Historical Review* 83 (December 1978): 1174-1175, quoted by Prema Kurien, "Becoming American by Becoming Hindu: Indian Americans Take Their Place at the Multicultural Table," in *Gatherings in Diaspora*, ed. Warner, 43.

44 Warner, *Gatherings in Diaspora*, 17.

45 Kurien, "Becoming American by Becoming Hindu," 45.

46 Kurien, "Becoming American by Becoming Hindu," 57.

47 Raymond Brady Williams, *A Sacred Thread: Modern Transmission of Hindu Traditions in India and Abroad* (New York: Columbia University Press, 1992), 239.

48 Kurien, "Becoming American by Becoming Hindu," 57.

49 Ritualistic sacrifice.

50 Kurien, "Becoming American by Becoming Hindu," 41-59.

51 During this time, indenture was a system of labor recruitment where the subject worked abroad and then returned to India once the terms of the contract were honored. This resulted in the formation of Indian communities in the plantation economies of Fiji, Malaysia, Mauritius, and British Guiana.

52 Helweg and Helweg, *An Immigrant Success Story*, 19-23.

53 Helweg, *An Immigrant Success Story*, 45.

54 Abraham, *The Asian Indian in the United States*, 9.

55 US Census Bureau, US Summary: 2000, Table DP-1, http://www.census.gov/prod/2002pubs/c2kprof00-us.pdf (accessed January 19, 2008).

56 Immigration Act of 1965, Public Law 89-236, *U.S. Statutes at Large* (1965).

57 Helweg, *An Immigrant Success Story*, 58-70.

58 Fenton, *Transplanting Religious Traditions*, 39.

59 Kurien, "Becoming American by Becoming Hindu," 42-43.

60 Helweg, *An Immigrant Success Story*, 23-38.

61 Rudrappa, *Ethnic Routes to Becoming American,* 110.

62 Helweg, *An Immigrant Success Story,* 11-17.

63 Abraham, *The Asian Indian in the United States,* 30.

64 Sodowsky, "Relationships between Acculturation-Related Demographics," 118, quoted in Abraham, *The Asian Indian in the United States,* 30.

65 Rudrappa, *Ethnic Routes to Becoming American,* 125.

66 Helweg, *An Immigrant Success Story,* 63, 66.

Two

Indericans - The Second
Generation - "Amy Patel"

The second generation is the most unique of all the Indian generations in America. The first generation – Enterans – are Indians that are transplanted into a different setting. The third generation of Indians is most likely to be completely American in nature. The Inderican, on the other hand, is torn between the world at home that is Indian and the world outside the home, which is American. Though there were Indericans from the late eighteenth century, this study is focused on the children of the Enterans that came to America in the post-1965 era.

THEIR INDIAN-NESS

Enteran parents initially are usually uncompromising in regard to Indian culture and practices. Their home could as well have been in India. The Indianness of the Inderican comes from the home in such a background and is seen in the following areas.[67]

In physical appearance, Indericans look like Indians. Until they talk, their Americanness is less obvious. Of course, there is an immediate, noticeable difference between the way Indericans and un-acculturated Enterans dress.

As to language, they speak their mother tongue at home and English outside. Thus, unlike most American classmates in elementary school, Indericans are able to converse in two or more languages. They may not know the Indian languages perfectly, but are comfortable enough for daily conversation.

Regarding attire, especially as children, Indericans are likely to be the odd ones out wearing clothes that cover almost every inch of their bodies. This tendency to be the odd one is a constant source of embarrassment to the Inderican. It is only later that they enjoy wearing Indian outfits on special occasions.

Music and movies watched depend on the Enterans' origin in India, as music and movies relevant to that particular language group is played and discussed at home. As a result of the lack of Indian contact for Enterans, they try to recapture memories of their time in India via these media. Thus, the Inderican grows up with Indian movies and/or music at home and is even able to name several actors or artists.

They eat Indian food at home, as least initially, and eat American food outside the doors of the house. Thus, they grow with their gustatory senses needing an increased level of spice to be satisfied. At least initially, find many American cuisines to be bland.

In the matter of religion, Enterans tend to maintain the religion with which they entered into the country. They, in turn, impart their religious views to their children. Since Hinduism is often equated with Indianness, Indericans fail to distinguish the extremely fine line between Indian culture and Hinduism, so that many Hindu practices are thought to be Indian.

As to family values, the Indian concept of the family unit is transmitted to the Inderican. The lives of Enteran parents revolve around their children. In fact, once their children are born, it is unthinkable for parents to go anywhere without their children. The mere contemplation of leaving their children for a few hours or a few days seems sacrilegious. Thus, Enteran parents do not go on dates or vacations without their children. The Indericans grow up being the center of the Indian family, and their relationships with their parents are, thus, very close knit.

In terms of respect for parents and elders, the authority of parents is recognized by children and invariably reminded by parents when needed. This reminding is necessary because of the potentially irreverent American context in which they live in. Children usually address their older siblings or cousins with a respective prefix or suffix and usually tend to maintain respect for those older than themselves. Enterans come from a culture where a younger person stands up in respect when an older person enters the room. This respect is not just for parents but for any older person, even if the age difference is only a few years.

Concerning the drive to succeed, Enterans came to America and had to start their lives all over. Thus, they were extremely driven to make a decent living and succeed at it. They realized that further education was necessary for them to rise in society, and they persevered in spite of the cultural differences and barriers. This attitude is instilled into their children, and they are told from a very early age what kind of profession and education they should be pursuing. This drive to pursue and succeed is, therefore, deeply embedded within the Inderican.

Indian parenting style and discipline are practiced in most homes....most parents will almost sacrifice anything to be of help and support to their children. Their expectation is so high that it reflects on the achievement level of the children. Most of them aim for higher education and higher professions.[68]

In marriage choices, from a very early age, Indericans are cautioned about the difficulties of marrying outside of the culture. They grow up with the view that no other relationship, except those with Indians, will be tolerated. Enterans can have an often fanatical opinion on this issue, especially during their early years in the country.

Marriage for the Indian is not just about two people getting together. It is about two families marrying each other, so it is important for the Indian family that the family that their children marry into be culturally compatible with them. Unfortunately, the curse of the caste system creeps into their opinions, so they tend to unconsciously rank the cultures around them. Thus, though relationships with certain cultures may eventually be accepted, relationships with other cultures can initially be deemed inexcusable.

In many homes, young people are not permitted to date or spend time outside of the house without parental permission; Indian boys are probably given more freedom than girls to be out of the house to run errands or engage in social activities. The parents also expect their children to stay with them until they are married and have sufficient income to live independently....

Prearranged marriages are not uncommon, but they do it with the consent of the youngster. Most parents expect their children to choose partners who belong to the same subculture or religious denomination. Asian Indians frown upon divorces just like in India, where it is almost a violation of ethical and spiritual codes of law.[69]

As Indericans get older, this topic accrues a lot of conversation time with Enterans finding it impossible to give concrete reasons why their children cannot date non-Indians and Indericans finding it impossible to understand the cultural aspects of a relationship. It is not unusual for Indericans to avoid dating from other cultures just to avoid a confrontation at home. As with all generalizations, there are always exceptions to the common.

Concerning their association with family in India, many Enterans have left behind families in India. Either immediate family members or members of the extended family reside in India. It is not unusual for Enterans, together with their children, to make a trip back to India once every few years. When the children are younger, the entire family goes. However, as the Indericans get older, it is more and more difficult to coordinate school and college schedules with parents' work schedules, and so the visits get further and further apart. Also, for children, the long journey and stay in India was a great alternative to staying at home during the summer vacation. However, as the children get older and are able to move around by themselves, they are less and less likely to voluntarily make a trip to India, except of course, in the case of a marriage, anniversary, or funeral.

Association with other Indians in America is important. Due to the Enterans' desire to maintain Indian culture, Indericans end up being associated with Indian organizations. Over time, especially if the parents started the practice in the early years, Indericans enjoy this contact with other Indians.

The nurturing community environment provided by the OHM[70] and the Bala Vihar also inculcates in the children a strong sense of subcultural affiliation and pride. Most of the teenagers who attended the meetings on a regular basis told me that they would prefer to marry a fellow ethnic, since such a person would best be able to relate to their family and their culture.[71]

THEIR AMERICAN-NESS

Inderican Americanness is seen in several areas, as well. Most Indericans do not have an accent when speaking English. In addition, even though many Indians speak English, there are many words or phrases that are characteristically Indian English. As Indericans grow up, since they are educated in American English, they are able to quickly identify the Indian English spoken by their parents.

In terms of cuisine, as Indericans grow up and eat more and more from outside the home (or, as Enterans get acculturated and attempt American foods at home), they are able to acquire a taste for non-Indian food, even though it is not as spicy or flavored as traditional Indian food. Regarding clothes, Indericans wear American clothes as they grow older and usually successfully convince their Enteran parents to do the same.

As to music and movies, it is truly impossible for the Inderican to grow up in American culture and not be exposed to American music and movies. Even though they thought highly of Indian movie stars during their growing years, once they start seeing American movies and listening to American music, it is very rare for them to return to Indian movies and music. In fact, they are only too willing to poke fun at their parents' continued interest in Indian movies.

Regarding the concept of independence, in a survey conducted among Indericans, 95 percent of them mentioned independence as being one of their American traits. Since American culture is more outgoing than Indian culture is, Americans tend to be extremely independent. They desire to make their own choices and legally are expected to do so once they turn eighteen, even if an eighteen-year-old is not mentally much more mature than a seventeen-year-old. As a result of American culture's establishing eighteen as the adult age and because of the possibility of governmental intrusion into a family's life for children under that age, American youth grow up thinking (and knowing) that no one, including parents, can force them to do anything. This contributes to the independence of Americans, which is reflected in the Inderican.

In communication, since Americans communicate a lot more than Indians do, that aspect spills over into the Inderican personality. However, this openness is not matched by the Indian-born Enteran. Enteran parents tend to give "orders" and expect their children to obey them without question. As Indericans grow older and start to have conversations concerning those "orders," the frequent sad result is confrontation. Indericans cannot understand why parents cannot talk things out and Enterans assume that any intention to talk out an "order" is a reflection of disrespect.

Regarding extracurricular activities, Indians in India generally do not have any. Enterans, therefore, carry on that feature, even in America. Their initial impulse is that education (book learning) is the most important and everything else is a waste of time. However, as Enterans go through their children's schooling, they realize that there are many more extracurricular activities and hobbies available to their children which were not available to them growing up and are more than willing to humor their children's desires as long as, in typical Indian outlook, it does not interfere with their education.

THEIR IDENTITY STRUGGLE

When the nature of the Inderican is separated into its bi-cultural components, it is relatively easy to comprehend the American parts and the Indian parts. However, these separate parts exist in the same person, and that is where the problem lies. There are certain areas in the identity of the Inderican where the American identity is in direct opposition to the Indian identity. This is the battlefield for the immigrant family. It is in these areas that the Inderican has to strike a delicate balance to avoid conflicts between his or her Indian family and his or her American friends. If the white areas are American and the black areas are Indian, this is the grey area – the area that present the largest and fiercest struggle for the Inderican. These are the areas over which there will be endless conversations and questions in the family and the awkward, if not sheepish, explanation to friends. As they grow older, Indericans tend to distance themselves from their parents' culture and identify more with the culture of their friends in school. There is always an issue of allegiance. They want to please their parents and be Indian, but they also want to please their friends and be American.

Indericans also have to deal with essential differences between the west and the east. There are psychological differences between the east and west.

In the west, the development of the individual identity is generally seen in socio-psycho-sexual-cognitive terms (Erikson, Freud, Piaget). The west values individualism, independence and innovation, while the eastern societies value community, interdependence and tradition. In eastern cultures like India, development of identity has a strong bearing on the surrounding community.[72]

There is a war within the Inderican – between the American side and the Indian side. Even though for some issues a compromise is essential, many times the Inderican chooses the American side or the Indian side. "But not all (Indericans) want to integrate everything; they are comfortable with discrete pieces of their identities. No single identity is able to define them completely. They constantly wrestle to hold on to every identity simultaneously."[73]

KINDS OF INDERICANS

There are four main groups in this interrelation.[74] First, there are *marginalists* – those with low Indian-ness and low American-ness (LILA). This group assimilates very little to either culture. They are critical of both cultures and tend to be severely marginalized. They are ashamed of their looks, skin color, and ethic features. They stay isolated from American culture and Indian communities. Some Indericans in their mid-teens, out of disillusionment, can fall into this category.

Next are *traditionalists* - those with high Indian-ness and low American-ness (HILA). This group is more Indian than American. They usually grow up in places where there is a high concentration of Indians and stay only within the Indian communities, churches, and temples. They tend to criticize the American culture, consider Indian culture to be superior to others, and refuse to consider themselves as Americans. They tend to maintain close ties with relatives in India; they speak Indian languages and have an Indian accent. They are most likely to marry Indians, many times in the traditional arranged marriage to someone from India. Indericans in their early teens fall into this category.

Third are *assimilationists* - those with low Indian-ness and high American-ness (LIHA). This group of people grew up primarily in a non-Indian setting and are very comfortable in associating with Americans. It is not unusual for them to be highly critical of Indian culture and practices and open to marrying non-Indians. Their knowledge of Indian languages and culture is very limited, and they have less contact with their relatives in India. Indericans in high school and college fall into this category.

Last are *biculturals* those with high Indian-ness and high American-ness (HIHA). This is a small group of Indericans who are comfortable in both Indian and American settings. They know both cultures and so are able to objectively choose the best of both cultures. They are comfortable marrying either Indians or a non-Indians, but less likely to marry someone directly from India.

ISSUES AFFECTED BY HYBRIDIZATION

Though this hybridization can affect almost every area of an Inderican's life, some of the crucial issues are detailed here.[75] One issue is marriage. Indericans are prevented from dating during their growing years, but still required to marry Indians.

The once cherished traditional family is breaking under the influence of American life style. More and more young people are engaging in mixed marriages, which are against traditional thinking. The first generation is almost at a point when they are afraid of losing their Indian identity and experiencing the collapse of everything they tried so hard to accomplish from the time they stepped on the adoptive land.[76]

Indericans vacillate in the dilemma of marrying an Indian in a custom that they are increasingly less familiar with and marrying a non-Indian, thus upsetting their parents.

Another issue is parental control. In the Indian family, parents have a say in their children's business, no matter how old they get. This is seen even when the Inderican is in college, away from parents, and over the age of eighteen. Indian parents do not believe that their eighteen-year-old child is an adult, and, in more ways than not, even basic adult decisions are difficult for this "adult" to make. The Indian parent knows this and therefore helps the adult child to make the decisions.

In terms of profession, there is a stereotype of what professions Indians are "supposed" to pursue. In the mind of Enteran parents, this stereotype is clear even before their child is born. Indericans are destined to attempt the professional paths laid out for them by their parents. It is not uncommon to see Indericans attempting the parental educational path and losing a few years in the attempt before the parents finally realize that their children need to make their own choices, lest they run the risk of not getting an education at all.

As to spirituality, many Indericans are torn between their parents' cultural religion and their own inner spiritual needs. In order to accommodate this, they continue to go with their parents to their places of worship or fellowship and then, on their own, go elsewhere so that their spiritual needs can be met.

THEIR RELIGIOUS OUTLOOK

Most of the religiosity of Indericans is similar to that of their American Generation X friends. The only difference is that the major religion is Hinduism instead of Christianity.

Institutions are suspect as many Indericans are suspicious of organized religion and willing to experiment with a collage of religions available. Tom Beaudoin, a Gen Xer himself, talks about the religious outlook of Xers.

Generation X approaches religion with a lived theology that is very suspicious of institutions. Indeed, they have a heavily ingrained (one could say constitutional) suspicion or skepticism (even cynicism) in general. This skepticism surfaces most acutely in regard to those who purport to be looking out for the generation's good. As the self-appointed guardians of souls, religious institutions are therefore frequent objects of GenX criticisms.[77]

In the relationship between culture and religion, Indericans dislike the fact that Enteran religion blurs the boundary between what is cultural and what is spiritual. Since Hinduism has been a part of Indian life for thousands of years, many cultural issues are considered to be religious and many religious aspects are considered to be cultural. There is no contradiction for the Enteran because Hinduism was a way of life for them in India. However, for Indericans who are detached from Indian life, the difference between Indian culture and Hinduism is starkly evident.

Another aspect of their religious outlook is the importance of experiences.

Xers generally find the religious in personal experience, particularly in an emerging form of sensual spirituality. In this turn to experience there is a constant yearning, both implicit and explicitly for the almost mystical encounter of the human and divine. This turn to experience also manifests in a new interest in communities of faith, as well as in faith lived in the everyday experience of the world.[78]

Xers will not simply accept religious truth instinctively from a religious authority. Whatever is claimed to be religious must meet the ultimate Gen X test: their personal experience.

Indericans and Xers hold to the centrality of ambiguity. Ambiguity is central to faith. Gen X can live with two contradictory ideas. They can be pro-choice in regard to abortion, for example, and pro-life in regard to whales and trees. They will also say they want a meaningful and lasting relationship with a lover, but, if someone better comes along, they would rather have him or her.[79] The Boomer was concerned with meaning of life issues. The question that the experiential Xer poses is a personal one: "Will you be there for me?"

We ask this of ourselves, bodies, parents, friends, partners, society, religions, leaders, nation, and even God. The frailty that we perceive threatening all of these relationships continually provokes us to ask this question....Xers start their fundamental questioning not with a grand quest for the meaning of their life but by querying those around them (including their "selves") in regard to their fidelity. Because these are boundary questions, informing the core of Gen X identity and giving shape to the limits of how we understand ourselves...they are ultimately religious questions.[80]

This ambiguity is seen in the merger between the east and the west.

Just as the western world is more guilt and performance oriented, the eastern world is more shame and being oriented. In the east, the public perception and communal thinking is far more valued than one's own conviction or individuality.... The social consequence of "getting caught" is seen as more important than the individual's feeling or the experience; defilement or contamination is a bigger issue than depravity itself...guilt tells me I made a mistake. Shame tells me that I am a mistake. If my behavior is wrong, I can correct it and change. If my very being is flawed, I am without hope for change.[81]

Indericans live in a different culture. They live in a culture that is both guilt and shame based.

Another feature of the religious terrain is non-sectarianism. The postmodern outlook of the Inderican desires a more ecumenical religion – one that is not divided into language of origin, or place of origin. It is difficult for Indericans to constantly have to separate themselves from their American friends so as to be a part of Indian religion. If they can go to school with their friends, then they prefer to go to worship with their friends, too. Indericans are disillusioned with the faith of their Enteran parents and prefer, in postmodern style, to cut and paste the best of all religions into one multifaceted religion that they can live in. They are more open toward other religions, having grown up in a setting where everyone from different backgrounds coexists.

Genuineness is another feature. Indericans need to see real faith, not an institutionalized, hypocritical, made-up religion. They are tired of their parents using religion for non-spiritual reasons and are drawn to a genuine seeking after God. They want to live out the faith, not just talk about it.

Lack of interest is found among some Indericans. Many early Enterans, on arriving in the United States, continued to live exactly as they did in India. One of the areas most affected as a result of this was religious transmission to Indericans. Since people in India are immersed in Hindu culture, very little effort was needed by parents to instill Hindu practices and beliefs. However, in a predominantly Christian American culture, those parents that put less effort into indoctrinating their children with the Hindu faith found that their children had very little desire for Hindu culture and practices and tended to be more secular and areligious. They went to religious events at the behest of their parents, merely for the social aspect. Indericans were, therefore, instilled with merely a general sense of god and religion without any specific direction in living it out. Later Enterans, or those Enterans that realized that they would be staying permanently in America, began to put in a concerted effort in imparting Hindu beliefs to their children.[82]

GENERATIONAL DIFFERENCES[83]

Indericans are different from Americans in their physiognomy, psychology, spirituality, individuality, community, and daily living. They are different from Enterans in many of the same aspects. A summary of their differences are listed in Table 2.1

Table 2.1. Differences between Enterans and Indericans

Enteran	Inderican
Identity is ascribed; family and caste related identity is imposed	Identity is achieved; familial and caste related identity is rejected
More communally minded	More individually minded
Individuals are viewed in terms of social hierarchy. Interpersonal relationships are formal with elaborate sense of rules	All persons are viewed equal. Interpersonal relationships are informal, flat without any complexities.
Social behavior caste and religion related	Social behavior class related
Roles are well defined, gender based	Roles are flexible and loosely defined
Religion plays a dominant role in everyday life	Less religious, yet more spiritual
Religious rituals play a crucial role in daily life	Rituals are mostly secular; religious rituals are less important
Tend to be fatalistic and superstitious	Tend to be rational, logical and needing explanation
Emotions are kept in check	Emotions are freely expressed
Flexible attitude to time	Rigid attitude to time
Goal and status driven	Relationship driven
Values uniformity	Values diversity
Leadership based on position and role	Leadership based on trust and relationship

Table 2.1 Cont'd.

Enteran	Inderican
Decision-making is directive, mostly made by those in authority and the rest are expected to follow	Decision-making is participatory. Involvement of everyone is appreciated. Democratic in nature. All inputs are considered for its worth
Use internet for information	Use internet for relationship
Communications with others are often indirect and contextual formal and planned	Communication with others is usually direct and to the point, informal and spontaneous
Emphasis on extended families	Prefers nuclear families, privacy and independence
Emphasis on collective responsibility and collective achievement	Emphasis on personal responsibility and individual achievement

Indericans are the most unique of all Indian generations in America. Their uniqueness arises from the fact that Indian culture refuses to syncretize with the existing American context. The main reason for this is the rich history of Indian culture that predates most other cultures. A unique generation requires a unique kind of evangelism to be reached.

Notes:

67 Several of the points mentioned are from conversations and surveys done among Indericans.

68 Abraham, *The Asian Indian in the United States*, 13.

69 Abraham, *The Asian Indian in the United States*, 12-13.

70 OHM (Organization of Hindu Malayalees) is a congregation of Hindu immigrants from the state of Kerala in South India. Bala Vihar is a child development organization culturally from Tamil Nadu (another Indian State). Both organizations are in the vicinity of Los Angeles, California.

71 Kurien, "Becoming American by Becoming Hindu," 61.

72 Sam George, *Understanding the Coconut Generation* (Niles, IL: Mall Publishing, 2006), 52.

73 George, *Understanding the Coconut Generation,* 60.

74 George, *Understanding the Coconut Generation,* 82-87.

75 Hybridization refers to the result of the complex union of the Indianness and Americanness in the Inderican. This union can manifest itself variously.

76 Abraham, *The Asian Indian in the United States,* 29.

77 Tom Beaudoin, *Virtual Faith* (San Francisco, CA: Jossey-Bass Inc., 2000), 52.

78 Beaudoin, *Virtual Faith,* 74.

79 Dieter Zander, "The Gospel for Generation X" in Marshall Shelley, ed., *Growing Your Church through Evangelism and Outreach* (Nashville, TN: Random House, Inc., 1996).

80 Beaudoin, *Virtual Faith,* 140-141.

81 George, *Understanding the Coconut Generation,* 78-79.

82 Fenton, *Transplanting Religious Traditions,* 217-227.

83 George, *Understanding the Coconut Generation,* 100-101.

Three

Religious and Cultural Influence of America on Indians

E very person lives in a culture, and, every person contributes to the culture. It is a symbiotic relationship. The person is influenced by culture, and culture is influenced by persons collectively. Thus, it is important to see both sides of the spectrum. When a person from another culture is transplanted to a new culture, both the culture and the person are slowly changed until there is a happy medium in which both co-exist – each dependent on the other.

SOME STRENGTHS OF THE AMERICAN CULTURE AS RELATED TO INDIANS

When Enterans came to America, and indeed continue to come, they were not disappointed. Most Enterans experienced an initial shock of seeing very few people on the streets and in neighborhoods when they are used to spatial invasion at home. Eventually they settled down to regular American life.

First, America is a *land of opportunity*. It is possible for anyone to pursue anything at any time. In India, once a person is twenty-five to twenty-seven years of age, he or she is basically set in a profession, having completed education during the past five to seven years. It is not so in America. Anyone can at any age choose to pursue education or any profession. Everyone has the opportunity to do anything. That is why Enterans who come to America well past college age are able to start in a completely different direction professionally and fare well.

Next, there is *freedom of religion* in America. Even though India is a democratic country, there is less freedom of religion. The majority religion is Hinduism, and so the few groups of Hindu fanatics continue to harass and persecute the minority Muslims and Christians. Fueled by the support of fundamental Hindu political parties, persecution has increased substantially in India in the last quarter of the twentieth century. The minority groups have very little say by way of objection to these attacks. In light of this, the freedom of religion afforded to Indians in America is poignant. Hindus find that, even though they are a minority group in America, they are still able to voice their opinions and fight for their rights.

Equality in America means the same opportunities and privileges are available equally for everyone. This is contrary to the situation in India where the caste system plays a dominant role. The caste system, the varieties of religions and sects of religions, and the different language groups all affect one's opportunities – either in education, profession, or relationships.

The ability to *start afresh* is a boon to some. There are some immigrants who are at a stage in their lives where they are at a complete standstill. There is no chance for them to progress in India. Examples of such people are widows, divorcees, and those not able to perform well academically. For them, they would rather be in America than in India. They are given the opportunity to start afresh, with no questions asked and usually with increased opportunities catered to their specific need.

America affords *privacy*. An advantage can also be a disadvantage. The close-knit social unit that each Indian is surrounded by is a boon in the midst of a tragedy. However, that same close-knit society can be extremely intrusive into personal space, so much so that the blurring of individual boundaries is the norm. Personal details are known by everyone in the society. The individualistic American society is a welcome place when someone needs space to recover from personal losses and failures.

America also provides *justice*. India, too, is a land of laws. However, because of the sheer enormity of the population and the lack of centralization of technology, the enforcement of those laws can be less than adequate. Thus, there is widespread corruption from the top of the highest office to the bottom of the lowest social unit. America is a land of laws that are enforced. There is corruption in America, too. However, when a corrupt person is exposed, whoever she or he may be, justice is meted out impartially. Not so in India. Very few convictions occur for those who are in power or are well connected or have disposable income. In general, there is nothing that money cannot buy in India, including justice.

SOME WEAKNESSES OF AMERICAN CULTURE AS RELATED TO INDIANS

There are, however, some aspects of American culture that are irreconcilable to the Indian mind. One involves *marriage and family values*. The lax rules pertaining to marriage relationships are frowned upon. Enterans caution Indericans about live-in relationships, the extended years of dating (which open doors for impiety), and the lack of commitment to hold on "till death do us part." The 50 percent rate of marriage breakdown is disconcerting to Enterans.

Another aspect is *sexuality*. American culture is more overtly sexual than Indian culture. Freedom of expression has unfortunately resulted in a break-down of traditional views of modesty. The focus on the individual has resulted in the permissiveness and acquiescence of individuals' fantasies. In contrast, for example, in India there are no R-rated movies. There is no profanity or nudity in general movies in India. (Pornographic movies are shown in exclusive porn theaters, but no adult material is shown in a theatre for the general public). Even movies from America that are shown in India are censored so that the of-fending scenes are deleted. There are no adult stores or strip clubs. The Enteran is rudely shaken to find this kind of sexual openness in America. In addi-tion, homosexuality and trans-sexuality are not yet an issue in Indian families. Enterans are still battling and trying to comprehend issues of heterosexuality. Homosexuality and trans-sexuality seem to be issues that are still far away.

Independence is an issue as Indians are codependent on each other. Even though American independence is appealing initially, its novelty quickly wears off. Independence appeals to young people. Enterans bemoan the culture of independence as their children get older and make their own choices. For parents who watch their children hurtling towards disaster and are unable to do anything because of the legal implications of independence, the concept is catabolic.

As to *relationships*, Indians find the American parent-child relationship baffling. The underlying theme is independence and individualism. Many American parents do not mind sending their children away from home once they turn eighteen, just so that parents can have their lives to themselves without being "burdened" by children. True, children want to leave the home too. Sadly, that karma returns when the child forces a parent to stay in a nursing home because the parent is now a hindrance to the child's life. In Indian families, parents want children (and children are expected) to live in the parents' house as long as they want, sometimes until marriage, sometimes even after marriage. When children move out, the parents stay alone until they cannot take care of themselves. At this time, *karma* (and sacrifice) returns, and parents move either with or very near their children, and the children take care of their parents.

Areligious beliefs are a concern. Indians are highly religious. The plurality of gods in Hinduism attests to this fact. Most Hindus even have a room in the house dedicated to their gods, called the *puja* room. America was a very religious country, but is becoming progressively secular. Living one's life completely and totally on one's strength and without the invocation of a higher power is unfathomable to the Indian mind.

Also of concern is the *lack of respect*. The traditional respect for elders and those in authority is lacking in America. The underlying issue is arrogance. Teachers in India are given the right to spank their students if need be. Whenever a teacher complains to parents about their children, the parents without question take the side of the teachers and punish their children. Children were disciplined if they showed even an iota of disrespect for any elder, including teachers, parents, and relatives. In contrast, parents in America defend their children against their teachers. This teaches the children that they do not need to respect authority. It comes full circle when those children turn around and disrespect their parents.

Racism is a factor. In spite of the protests to the contrary, in a post-civil rights America, Indians faced racism when they immigrated. Since the initial Enterans who emigrated for professional reasons were seen as a model minority due to their higher education and high average income, these Enterans largely ignored the racism that was directed at them so as to maintain equilibrium and not upset the status quo.[84]

INFLUENCE OF AMERICAN CULTURE ON THE ENTERAN[85]

Once Enterans get past jet lag after their arrival to the United States, they have to deal with both a completely new culture and homesickness. These two aspects are usually inversely proportional. The more acculturated Enterans get to American culture, the less homesick they will be.

First was a welcome. From the ease of applying for immigration to the welcome letter that most Enterans received from the Department of Homeland Security, Enterans were welcomed to America. Enterans came from a country that existed before history books were conceived. Thus, Indians lived in India all the time without any need for anyone to welcome anyone else. India is not a land made up of immigrants like America is. America is hence welcoming to immigrants and makes them feel at home.

They can enjoy the diversity of occupations. Enterans can start their lives any time they choose because of the opportunities available to anyone of any age. America is a land of choices, and that extends even to education and careers. There is a larger variety of careers to choose from. In addition, one can get more income for the same work with the ability to make one's own life in one's own way.

Female independence is an influence. Enterans come from a culture that is more patriarchal than egalitarian. However, when they come to America, women find that they are given the freedom to do virtually everything that a man can do. This independence of Indian women is immediately noticed by visitors from India.

There is enjoyment of life. Enterans have lived on both sides of immigration. For many Enterans, life in America is much more organized and convenient than life in India. The amenities available to each household, on average, are more than what is available on average in Indian houses. In addition, Americans enjoy life more than Indians in general. The average person in India has fewer hobbies, does not travel much, and never takes vacations. Enterans eventually learn to enjoy life, both as a result of American influence, and as a way to unwind from stressful work situations.

In terms of higher education, it is easier to pursue higher education in America than in India. There are several reasons for this. Even though education in America is expensive, it is easier to get financing for it. There are federal loans available. In addition, age is not a limiting factor for education, and there are plenty of options for long distance education and partial credit education too.

In terms of parenting, Enteran parents have changed their discipline of their children slightly. In keeping with the laws of America, parents are more hesitant to physically punish their children. Terms like "timeout" and "psyche" have become part of parenting vocabulary.

There is also an expanded worldview. Enterans grew up with an eastern worldview. The eastern and western worldviews are very different. That difference is shrinking with the progress of communication and the localization of the world. Still, there is a difference. Enterans are blessed with the opportunity of starting their life with one worldview and ending it in another context – the western worldview.

In terms of social skills, Enterans in general are socially awkward (except for those who were naturally hyper-extroverts). The main reason for this is the diversity of languages in India and the social barriers to conversation. For example, in rural settings, women do not engage in conversation with men they do not know. In urban settings, the main hindrance to random conversation with a stranger is usually the multiplicity of languages spoken. In an American context where everyone greets each other in English and everyone can converse with everyone else, Enterans learn to be more socially open than they were when they came to the country.

There is a liberal tendency. Enterans arrive with certain inhibitions, but, as time goes along, they feel fewer taboos regarding certain topics like sexuality or specific male or female issues that are part of common conversation in America. In addition, in spite of the views Enterans grew up with, when they come to America, the permissive, hypersexual culture subconsciously permits more affairs and divorces. Divorce is not frowned upon in America as it is in India.

INFLUENCE OF AMERICAN CULTURE ON THE INDERICAN

Even though Indericans are born into Indian families, eventually the American culture exerts its constant, powerful influence. Regarding occupational opportunities, the gamut of choices is wide in America. There are numerous branches that someone can major in, including the arts. However, Indericans will be involved in many heated conversations with their parents regarding their career choice and why they refuse to go down the career path their parents have chosen for them.

As to social strengths, Indericans grow up mingling with different cultures, languages, and races of people and know how to deal with them. Thus, there is openness to new ideas and opinions. Indericans are more accepted in American society since, apart from the physiognomic features, there is very little external difference between them and Americans, including the lack of an accent. For this reason, it is not uncommon for Enteran parents to ask their children to talk to customer service or order in a drive-through.

Indericans experience slow maturity. In general, Enterans matured quickly because of the increased responsibilities that they had in migrating, settling down in a new country, and relearning a whole new system of living. Enterans subsequently worked hard to ensure a good life for their children. Indericans came along without any knowledge of the hardships that their parents had gone through to give them the good life. That good life resulted in a decrease in responsibility and an entitlement mentality. They were given everything that they wanted and assume that they will get everything that they want from life, only to rudely realize that life is not as forgiving.

Regarding Christianity, American culture is undoubtedly a Christian culture. Even though Christian days like Good Friday and Christmas are national holidays in India, since the major religion is Hinduism, Indian culture revolves around Hindu holidays. Indericans growing up in a Christian culture celebrate Christian holidays and seasons, of course with no spiritual involvement. It is not surprising to find a Christmas tree in a Hindu house during Christmas time.

Lastly, there is a lack of Indian connection. In spite of the Enterans' strong attempts to inculcate Indian-ness into their children, as they become older, they have less connection with India. They may know some words in an Indian language, may remember some Indian movies, and may like some Indian foods, but eventually the American culture overpowers a long-distance Indian influence. The busyness of American life, the length of the journey to India (about twenty hours), and the difficulty in coordinating vacation schedules results in older Indericans seldom traveling to India. It is just a matter of time, then, before the Inderican becomes predominantly American.

HINDUISM IN AMERICA

The modern period of Indian history is when Hinduism finally made its way to America. A variety of reform movements developed around the time of India's independence in 1947. The most important of these was the Ramakrishna Mission, established by Swami Vivekananda. He spread the message of his guru, Ramakrishna, who had several extraordinary mystical experiences. Vivekananda developed a kind of monistic Vedanta philosophy that believes that all reality is united in Brahman,[86] and combined it with social action. He came to Chicago for the World Parliament of Religions in 1893 and made a deep impression with his oratory skills. He traveled widely in the United States and made many American converts.[87]

IMPORTANT DATES OF HINDUISM IN AMERICA[88]

Even though Hindus came to North America in the early part of the eighteenth century, Hinduism was considered to be a primitive religion of a pagan people that lived far away. It was in 1893 when Swami Vivekanada came to the World Parliament of Religions at Chicago and gave a talk uninvited that Hinduism was placed on a world stage. Table 3.1 lists the key moments in the history of Hinduism in America.

Table 3.1. Hindu history in America

When	Who	What they did
1893	Swami Vivekananda	Speaks at the World Parliament of Religions at Chicago and introduces Hinduism to America.
1894 and 1899	Swami Vivekananda	Established Vedanta societies in New York and San Francisco
1920	Paramhansa Yogananda	He came to Boston to attend a conference of the Unitarian Church. He subsequently founded the Self-Realization Fellowship that was the largest Hindu organization with two hundred thousand members till the 1960s.
1930s and 1940s	Aldous Huxley, Gerald Heard and Christopher Isherwood	They emigrated from Britain to the US and revived Vedanta philosophy.
1950s	Sivaya Subramuniyaswami	A US convert to the Saiva Siddhanta Church in India, he returned to the US and established headquarters in Kauai, Hawaii. This organization publishes a current newspaper, Hinduism Today.
1959	Maharishi Mahesh Yogi	He founded an offshoot of Hinduism called Transcendental Meditation and attracted many followers, including the Beatles and Mia Farrow.
1966	Abhay Charan De (aka Swami Prabhupada)	He established the International Society for Krishna Consciousness – ISKCON. When he died eleven years later, he had personally converted 5000 Krishna worshippers.

Many of these organizations and movements introduced a missionary type of Hinduism. The new age movement included Hindu mysticism, and many Americans were drawn into the new experience. The main point, however, is that Hinduism became international, and Hindu terms became part of the colloquial language. Even though many people were converted to these branches of Hinduism, currently the majority of Hindus are those that have emigrated from India.

AMERICANIZATION OF HINDUISM

Hinduism in America is not an exact replication of Hinduism in India. It is inevitable that the American culture would influence any immigrant belief, especially Hinduism, because of its potent malleability. Three of the main adaptations of Hinduism to American culture are given below.[89]

Ecumenization

Hinduism in India is divided by language, sects, and geography. The beliefs of Indian Hinduism are so vast and convoluted that there is no one systematic theology written or articulated. When Hindus came to America, there were not enough of them to maintain those divisions. The few Hindus were spread across America from the East Coast to the West Coast. In addition, they were asked about their beliefs by curious Americans. It then became necessary to be able to formulate a creed applicable to the majority of Hinduism. This forced an ecumenical type of Hinduism that rose above the different sects in India. Thus, the general beliefs of American Hinduism were more homogenized. Also, since they wanted to make Hinduism more acceptable to Americans, who so far considered Hinduism to be a crude pagan religion, they modified some of their beliefs to fit the American context. Thus the caste system was denied, importance of women was highlighted, polytheism gave way to monotheism, and reason replaced superstition.

These are the nine major beliefs of Hinduism put forward by an American Hindu organization known as the Himalayan Academy.[90] First, Hindus believe that there is one, all-pervasive Supreme Being who is both immanent and transcendent. Second, Hindus believe in the divinity of the four *Vedas*, the world's most ancient scripture. Third, Hindus believe that the universe undergoes endless cycles of creation, preservation, and dissolution. Fourth, Hindus believe in *karma*, the law of cause and effect. Fifth, Hindus believe that the soul reincarnates, evolving through many births until all *karmas* have been resolved, and *moksha*, liberation from the cycle of rebirth, is attained. Not a single soul will be lost. Sixth, Hindus believe that divine beings exist in unseen worlds and that temple worship, rituals, sacraments, and personal devotionals create a communion with these *devas* and Gods. Seventh, Hindus believe that an enlightened master, or *satguru,* is essential for one's personal and spiritual life. Eighth, Hindus believe that all life is sacred and, therefore, practice *ahimsa*, noninjury, in thought, word, and deed. Finally, Hindus believe that no religion teaches the only way to salvation above all others, but that all genuine paths are facets of God's Light.

Congregationalization

Hindus in India visit temples only sporadically. Since most of them have a *puja* room in their house, it is mainly for Hindu festivals and special occasions that Hindus go to the temple. Since the majority of the country is Hindu, none of them suffers from the lack of communion with fellow Hindus. This is not the case in America.

Thus, American Hindus go to the temple more often so that they can meet other Hindus. The social element is as important as the religious one. Temples in America have become more than just a religious place; they are also social and cultural symbols.

Ritual Adaptation

Hinduism is intricately connected to the universe, namely nature. Many beliefs and rituals are astrological and thus have chronologic and diurnal variation. However, when that belief system is part of the American culture, it needs to follow the rigors of the American workweek, the holiday schedule, and available resources.

Thus, it is impossible for Hindus to follow every astrological intonation precisely. It is not possible for any Hindu to follow the sixteen life-cycle rituals *(samskaras)*, and they get to perform only a few of them that they think are the most important. For example, the American crematorium cannot hold the same sacredness as a funeral pyre on the banks of any revered Indian river.

Hinduism in America Today

Hinduism is no longer a fringe religion. More and more Americans are becoming aware of it and are able to recognize a traditional Hindu as a Hindu. The ever-accepting arms of American culture are slowly accepting Hindu terms and concepts as its own. Thus, the Hindu terms yoga, guru, avatar, and nirvana are in common use.

The last three decades have seen tremendous growth in the presence of Hindus in the United States. Most metropolitan cities have Hindu temples, and Hindu centers are found everywhere....it is estimated that 1.4 million people of Indian origin live in the United States; of these more than 85% (1.2 million) are Hindus.[91]

There are five types of Hinduism in America today.[92] Secular Hinduism includes those Hindus who do not identify with any specific doctrines or practices of traditional Hinduism, but have chosen not to affiliate with any other religion. Many educated Hindus fall into this category. Non-sectarian Hinduism embraces those Hindus that do not subscribe to any particular sect of Hinduism but practice a general kind of Hinduism. Many of these Hindus come from the Brahmin class. *Bhakti* Hinduism includes those Hindus who identify themselves with a particular sect in Indian Hinduism, for example vaishnavas and shaivas. Nationalist Hinduism holds those Hindus that still maintain allegiance to national Hindu organizations back in India. Missionary Hinduism refers to Neo-Hindu groups that sprung up, designed to appeal not only to the national audience but to an international audience as well.

Common features of these "export" or missionary brands of Neo-Hinduism include (1) devotion to a deified guru; (2) total obedience to the will or the guru; (3) the practice of one or another type of yoga; (4) the claim that all religions are basically valid; (5) the claim that one's national or ethnic identity has no bearing on the practice of the particular Neo-Hindu tradition; and (6) a tendency to de-emphasize social work or political activity of any kind.[93]

Some of these organizations that developed are: Self-Realization Fellowship in Los Angeles, Center of Satya Sai Baba, Spiritual Regeneration Movement or Transcendental Movement, ISKCON and Siddha Yoga. Hindus in this class are those that belong to the new age movement like the Hare Krishna Movement and Transcendental Meditation movement. These people are different from the other groups in that they actively seek to convert non-Hindus to their beliefs.

One of the strategies used by Hinduism to adapt to American culture is by emulating Jewish Americans. Jews in America are different from most other religious groups that migrated to America in that they merged into mainstream American culture but at the same time maintain their exclusiveness. In their attempt to so imitate Jewish Americans, Hindus started by forming anti-defamation groups that protested any attempt by the written, visual, or auditory media to defame Hindu beliefs and practices.[94] Other Hindu groups were formed that focused on getting Hinduism to be acknowledged as an American religion.[95] Thirdly, Hindu groups began to participate in inter-faith dialogues so as to present to America an Americanized Hinduism. In doing this, Hindus countered three main areas in which they were viewed negatively: they claimed that Hinduism was essentially a monotheistic religion based on early Vedas, that the caste system was never really accepted by Hinduism, and that women were not treated as sub-class citizens as was generally thought; rather they were held in as much esteem as men.[96]

Hindu adaptation to American Culture took an abrupt turn after the events of September 11, 2001. Before this, they tried to get the recognition that Islam and Judaism were getting from American culture. After the attacks on America, Hindus made a strong attempt to show themselves to be a peace loving religion and distance themselves from both Islam and Sikhism as they feared marginalization from the mainstream media. They worried about the unavoidable American camaraderie with Pakistan and attempted to use the rise of the anti-Islamic attitude in America to finally obtain the attention that they craved.[97]

Notes:

84 Chad Bauman and Jennifer Saunders, "Out of India: Immigrant Hindus and South Asian Hinduism in the United States" (research paper, College of Liberal Arts and Sciences, Faculty Scholarship, Butler University, 2009).

85 Many of these points were from conversations and surveys done among Indericans and Enterans.

86 That believes that all reality is united in Brahman.

87 Gerald James Larson, "Hinduism in India and in America" in Jacob Neusner, ed., *World Religions in America*, 4th ed. (Louisville, KY: Westminster/John Knox Press, 2009), 193-194.

88 Gurinder Singh Mann, Paul Numrich, and Raymond Williams, *Buddhists, Hindus and Sikhs in America: A Short History* (New York: Oxford University Press, 2008), 43-59.

89 Bauman and Saunders, "Out of India."

90 Adapted from http://www.hinduismtoday.com/modules/wfchannel/index.php?wfc_cid=19. (accessed November 7, 2009).

91 Madasamy Thirumalai, *Sharing Your Faith with a Hindu* (Minneapolis, MN: Bethany House, 2002), 12.

92 Adapted from Larson, "Hinduism in India and in America," 196-197.

93 Larson, "Hinduism in India and in America," 194-195.

94 For example, American Hindus Against Defamation (AHAD), Hindu International Council Against Defamation (HICAD) and www.indiacause.com.

95 They gained success for their labors – in September 2000 a Hindu priest opened a Congress session.

96 Prema A. Kurien, "Multiculturalsm and 'American' Religion: The Case of Hindu Indian Americans," *Social Forces* 85, no. 2 (December 2006): 730-731.

97 Kurien, "Multiculturalsm," 733-734.

Four

Analysis of Churches in America in Relation to Evangelism Among Indians

LESSONS FROM EVANGELISTIC EFFORTS OF THE AMERICAN CHURCH AMONG INDIANS

Most churches do not have an outreach program specific for Indians. Indeed, most churches do not have any outreach program toward any other minority groups in the country. Herb Miller gives ten reasons why churches do not emphasize evangelism in general: lack of theological motivation, failure to see that the factors that influence people to attend a church the first time are different from those that influence them to return and join the church, undue concentration on its inactive members, shift in focus from making disciples to serving disciples (making people more Christian and making more people Christian are as different as are obstetrics and pediatrics), the myth that spiritual growth is more important than numerical growth, not recognizing the high percentage of unchurched people, mentality that expects people to come to them without any inducing, the fallacy that merely letting your light shine is good enough, plain selfishness, and the apparent hesitation to become involved in the numbers game without realizing that people are numbers and God was interested in people and therefore in numbers.[98]

THE AMERICAN CHURCH

As far as the American church is concerned, Indericans are culturally more like them; it is the Enteran that is different and, hence, the need for a specific outreach. Every church attracts non-Christians who are most like the existing members. Thus, the ideal way for a church to attract Indians would be if there were already Indian/Hindu members in the church. The question then becomes how a church can attract a few Hindus who will, in turn, progressively attract other Hindus. Thus, getting the "pioneer" converts into the church is key for further growth of those particular people groups in the church, and the important question is how to attract pioneer Hindu converts into the church. This can take place only on an individual basis, via personal evangelism. Hence, the conversation with the Hindu co-worker around a coffee machine and that with the Hindu classmate around a school desk become substantially important. It is in these personal, conversational opportunities that American Christians have been less aggressive in introducing Jesus to Hindus. There are several reasons for this.

Firstly, Caucasian Christians and Enteran Hindus are at polar opposites. There is no cultural, religious, physiognomic, linguistic similarity between the two. The only factors binding the two classes is the English language, in spite of the obvious initial difficulty in understanding each other, and the professional expertise, which they both share. Thus, if a Caucasian pastor is trying to reach out to an Indian Hindu, the only similarity is English.

Secondly, a pastor trying to reach Enterans in the last quarter of the twentieth century was dealing with extremely qualified Indian immigrants, who were articulate professionals, mainly in computing and healthcare. Even though the relatives of Enterans after 1965 were not as qualified, American churches were forced to deal with an educated minority. Thirdly, the lack of knowledge of Hindu beliefs and practices and of Indian culture in general was a formidable barrier to reaching out to them. Since Hinduism did not have a concrete set of specific beliefs, it was hard to have even a general idea to classify Hinduism into philosophical or doctrinal categories.

Fourthly, the needs of the Enteran were vastly different from what the American church was prepared to and had the resources to fulfill. Fifthly, the lack of a sustained effort to reach out, specifically to this group of people, further shunted any efforts from coming to concrete fruition. Evangelism among Indians requires more patience and time. It requires less time and effort to talk to and meet the needs of an American individual. However, the Enteran is not just an individual. He or she is connected to a very close-knit family unit. Thus, evangelism directed at the individual was really for the whole family – usually the whole extended family – and so patient prayer, continued conversations, and waiting are key elements.

THE INDIAN CHURCH

The Indian church in America is not without culpability either. Indeed, it needs to be held more accountable. Following are the glaring aberrations.

There is no vision. Many Indian churches did not have an evangelistic vision. They were inward looking, trying to create a community that they had left behind in India. This, unfortunately, is a reflection of the inward looking church in India. Thus, they did not attempt to reach out to Hindus with intent. Church growth in most Indian churches occurs mainly because of biological growth, transfer growth, and immigration. There is really no emphasis on evangelism.

There is a non-recognition of Indericans. There is a false conception, which has been carried over from India, that the younger generation is just kids and that they eventually will learn to act like adults. Thus, there is very little done to minister to the younger generation. Most of the church's resources are allocated to minister to the older adults, exactly as in churches in India, in this case for the Enteran. Many times, the Indian Church completely ignores the spiritual needs of the Inderican.

Ignorance of the Inderican generation is another factor. Most Indericans who still persist at Indian churches agree that the spiritual input they get is very little. They initially get social and cultural needs met but rarely get their spiritual needs met. Eventually, as their burning need for the spiritual overcomes the social and cultural satisfaction these churches provide, they venture to other non-Indian churches.

There is also segregation of Indian churches along the lines of language and cultural divisions as they existed in India. This is acceptable as long as the intended audience is Enterans. However, this exclusion is contrary to the inclusive worldview of the postmodern, intercultural, non-Indian-language-speaking Inderican.

Culturalization is an issue, as well. The lines between tradition, culture, and biblical faith are blurred. Many Indian churches enforce tradition as biblical truth and disown some cultural aspects as unbiblical. Sam George says that the Christianity of many of the Indian churches makes it difficult to draw the line between culture and faith. They practice a culturized Christianity, invariably propagating Indian culture in the name of God....the church becomes the socialization vehicle to nurture the next generation in the culture and not necessarily biblical faith. Sometimes behaving the Indian way takes precedence over the Christian or even the biblical way. Sometimes it is reinforced in the name of tradition and with unflinching zeal to preserve it from adulteration from American Christianity.[99]

There is ignorance of the host culture, as well. Indian churches continue to look inward and fight amongst themselves over petty issues while completely ignoring and disdaining the American culture in which they live. They cannot preach a relevant gospel if they continue to ignore the context of that gospel.

The American church deals with problems the same way that corporate America deals with them – directly, analytically, and objectively. They analyze the problem; find solutions to it; consider the risks, benefits, and alternatives; and then make a firm decision, irrespective of the consequences, irrespective of the few who may be affected badly by it. Indian churches, on the other hand, will deny, then cover up, then ignore the problem until it is blown out of proportion. Then they will try to solve it without offending anyone, resulting, over a period of time, in many people in these churches, who are sucking the life out of them and should not be in those churches.[100] Many Indian churches contain multiple groups of factions owing allegiance to different people. This results in week after week in which church members are fighting against each other instead of trying to reach those who are outside of it. This takes place in full view of its Inderican youth, who progressively become disillusioned until they eventually leave. At this point, the Enteran church members criticize the indiscipline of the Indericans, and everybody loses.

FACTORS THAT HINDER EVANGELISM AMONG INDIANS

Christianity is a missional faith. Evangelism is not an option the church has. The church is one generation away from extinction if not for evangelism. As a result, Christian missionaries from Christian countries went all over the world, including India, to share the good news about Jesus. In that context, it would be expected that, when Hindus came to a predominantly Christian country, there would be widespread evangelism directed toward Hindus. But this is not the case.

Evangelism among Hindus is not being accomplished to its full potential. There are several factors that prevent effective evangelism among Hindus. First is fear of being insensitive. In a stunning reversal of the attitudes of some western evangelists to India in the centuries past, the issue is no longer that evangelists will be insensitive, but that the right thing will not be said because of the need to be politically correct.

There is ignorance of Hinduism. Most people in America, including both Indians and non-Indians, have an inadequate view of Hinduism. Many times that view is skewed to one of two extremes: either people think that Hinduism is one of the ways to heaven, or they categorize it as a demonic, pagan religion with no good in it. Both views are erroneous and extreme. A church that attempts to minister to Hindus should first learn an overview of Hinduism.

There is also ignorance of Indian culture. American churches assume that Indians, like many other foreign immigrants, want to assimilate into the American culture and so deal with them in an American way, but this is not true. Enterans do not want to assimilate culturally. Indericans come from a background with that viewpoint. Indian churches, on the other hand, fail to understand the American-ness of the Inderican and expect them to be Indian.[101] Thirty percent of churches surveyed said that they did not have sufficient knowledge of Indian culture to minister exclusively to them.

The accommodation of Hinduism, inherent in its nature, resists evangelistic attempts. Tirumalai evaluates Hinduism as the most accommodating of all religions. In a world full of strife, the "accommodative" spirit and the

plants of universalism and relativism, as well as the other cultivated characteristics of modern Hinduism, become very attractive to so many diverse groups
of people that the Hindus have truly come to see their faith as a relevant global
religion. This sense of importance, as well as pride in the ancestral past, continues to help encourage the intellectual Hindu to hold on to his religion and
resist the invitation of Christ.[102]

Changing theology in Christianity is another factor. There is an increasing
trend for some Christian leaders to consider that salvation can be obtained
other than exclusively through Jesus Christ. The increasingly accepted postmodern relativity leads to the subtle belief that there are many ways that lead
to God and Jesus is one of them. Thus, the emphasis and passion to reach out
to non-Christians naturally diminishes.

There is also a lack of time. Ten percent of the respondents said that lack
of time precludes evangelistic attempts among Indians. Additionally, there is a
lack of available people. Forty-seven percent of the respondents said that there
were not enough people who would lead such a ministry. In addition, several
churches said that they do not focus on reaching any one particular ethnic
group and try to reach out to as many groups as possible. One church said
that, even though they do not have any mission work directed among Indians
in America, they support missionary work in India.

FACTORS IN THE CHURCH THAT WOULD TURN INDIANS OFF

The church of today is different from the ministry of Jesus who went around
to the people. Today the church is in one location and invites people to come
to it. Thus the attendance in the church is dependent on the attractiveness of
the church and its message. There are some issues about the American church
that is not attractive for Indians.

Enterans

Irrelevant sermons are a hindrance. The needs of Enterans are different than the
needs of Caucasians. Thus, it is highly likely that a sermon directed toward a

predominantly Caucasian congregation would be irrelevant to an Enteran family. In addition, some of the topics that are discussed in the American church are not appealing to Indian families. For example, a sermon on sex, porn, and sexual relations within a marriage would make Enterans very uncomfortable.

Large churches can sometimes turn Enterans off. This is because Enterans prefer to enter into a deeper relationship with people, in contrast to the perceived superficiality of American relationships. Americans are more likely to make a cursory greeting than Enterans are. Enterans are, however, more likely to ask a personal question because they are more interested in deeper relationships than superficial ones. However, in a big church, there is less opportunity for deeper relationships. One is more likely to meet completely different people every week with no opportunity for deep fellowship.

Language and accent can be a problem. Some Enterans initially do not go to American churches because they either do not understand English well or, as is usually the case, they do not understand the American accent well. Many times, the Caucasian accent is easier to understand than the African-American accent. Lack of other Indians can also be an issue, mainly for Enterans. Thus, Indian churches are more equipped to attract Enterans than American churches are.

Lack of respect in church sometimes offends. Hindus come from a very respectful and respecting culture. Respect is given to elders, parents, those in authority, and God. When Hindus go to a temple they remove their footwear when they walk into the presence of their gods. They fear and are in awe of their gods. Christians behave very differently. Many of them do not show any signs of respect or awe of the God they worship. It is possible that God is less feared by Americans than by Indians. Similarly, lack of modesty is an issue. Enterans have their bodies covered more than Americans. This is especially true when Hindus go to a place of worship. They are prone to feel embarrassed if they see a worship team member not appropriately dressed.

Indericans
Indericans have grown up under the shadow of Enterans all their lives. In the church, Indericans were not considered to have a say in any matter. They

were dismissed as being just kids. As a result of the patriarchal background, Indian parents in India do not give much credence to young people's opinions or views. They were asked and expected to grow up and become like their parents. The same attitude continued in America. The only difference is that Indericans would never become like their parents.

Indericans who grew up without being respected usually tend to distance themselves from all that their parents believe in, including spiritual matters. Many Indericans who grew up in churches drop out of Indian churches when they get the chance, and they do it for several reasons. These are the top opinions Sam George found regarding why Indericans drop out of churches.

I don't get anything out of it.

Church is a club.

Church is full of hypocrites.

More interested in my money than me.

Politics in church.

Lack of engaging and relevant music/sermons.

Lack of authenticity.

Dull and boring.

Unfriendly to visitors and small children.

Other good alternative churches.[103]

FACTORS IN THE CHURCH THAT WOULD ATTRACT INDIANS

There are several factors in a church that can attract Indians in general and Hindus in particular. First is other Indians. In the survey conducted, the predominant opinion was that Indians would come to a church if there were other Indians in the congregation since like attracts like. The church should then focus on those "pioneer" Indians who would eventually be the stimulus for other Indians to start coming to church. Indians would also be attracted if there was an Indian on the pastoral staff or on the speaking team, especially from a scientific or technical background.

Indian-specific ministry would be attractive. Only a ministry that was specific to Indians or to Hindus will be able to understand and fulfill the needs of that particular people group. Obviously, the burden of this particular task falls upon all Indian churches in America. Also attractive is a worship service that gives a sense of the holy. This aspect is especially appealing to those *Bhakti* Hindus that are desirous of having their spiritual needs satisfied.

Friendliness would be important. Indians in general are not cordial with other Indians. Hence, when one Indian sees another Indian at the mall, they are more likely to stare and less likely to have a conversation. The reason for this is that, as a result of the multiplicity of languages, it is hard to gauge what language the other person speaks or from what subculture the other person comes. However, since everybody appreciates a smile and a hello, Indians, like other people, are attracted to a church that genuinely welcomes them. In addition, since many Enterans have faced and continue to face different shades of racism, friendliness opens doors. Almost 25 percent of churches surveyed said that friendliness would attract Indians.

A focus on the family is important. Since Indians are a family-based culture, any focus on the family including parenting seminars and ministries relevant to children will be attractive. Also, prayer and meditation are valued. Hinduism is, in general, a meditative religion, especially for those that follow the *Jnana Marga*. Thus, even though silent meditation is difficult for the fast moving American, for a Hindu it is easier to spend time in silent meditation and prayer. Other factors are mentioned in the list of spiritual gifts that would be relevant to Indians.

SPIRITUAL GIFTS IN THE CHURCH RELEVANT TO INDIANS

All spiritual gifts are for the edification of the church. However, some spiritual gifts are more effective in ministering to those from a traditional Hindu background. Hinduism is a karmic, ancient, language-based, pantheistic religion that respects ancestors to invoke their spirits. Thus, they benefit more from some gifts than from others.

Teaching and preaching are relevant. An in-depth study of the Scriptures is unknown to regular Hindus. Only Hindu priests engage in a study of

Hindu scriptures. Hindus care more about the teaching of the Bible than about the hierarchy of the Church. Seventy percent of those surveyed said that strong teaching of the word is very important to Indians.

Service is important, too. Sixty-five percent of those surveyed said that acts of compassion and the showing of mercy would be relevant to evangelism among Indians. Even though Hindus in general are a compassionate people, because of the law of *karma* that each one gets what he or she deserves, there is a tendency to be lackadaisical in the face of others' suffering. This is true in many parts of India. Thus, acts of service with no strings attached are a great attraction for Hindus.

Prophecy is valued. The superstitious nature of Hinduism desires to know and affect the future. Thus, an emphasis on the gift of prophecy and the prophetical aspects of Scripture is appealing to the Hindu mind. Hindus continue to seek astrologers in order to know the future, even when things do not happen the way it was predicted. In this context, the surety of biblical prophecy will validate the message of salvation.

Healing is attractive. Hindus are intrigued by the powers of healing. Due to their religious and karmic nature, sickness and health are seen as having a purpose and as being related to a higher being. Thus, Hindus invoke the favor of gods to avoid disease. The power of the Jesus over sickness and disease, then, is a powerful testimony to the message. In addition, spirit possession is a regular part of some aspects of Hinduism.

Spirit possession is a state of consciousness induced in a person by an alien spirit, demon, or deity; another personality takes control and the person is often not fully conscious when such a takeover occurs. In spirit possession, the person possessed shows a dramatic change in physical appearance, actions, voice, and manner, and frequently he or she remembers nothing of the possession. Behavior varies according to the kind and number of spirits that take possession. Spirit possession is a common phenomenon among Hindus..... Hindu women have always been spirit possessed in greater numbers than Hindu men. Traumatic life experiences open doors to seek the help of spirits, which in turn cause their own trauma. ... Hinduism does encourage spirit possession, and ... many Hindus seek the help of spirits for divination, healing and material prosperity.[104]

Unfortunately, those spirits themselves cause bondage, the bonds of which can be broken in the name of Jesus.

ENTRY POINTS AVAILABLE FOR INDIANS TO GET CONNECTED INTO A CHURCH

The church in America is increasingly immersed in a secular context. Visitors to the church are not familiar with church functions and church practices. It is more so with Hindus, who do not know anything about the church, many of them never having seen the inside of a church. Thus, it is highly unlikely that a Hindu would randomly choose to come to a church on a given weekend. The only way to attract Hindus to a church is through entry points. These are points that are connected to the church but serve a function in the community. They are mediators between the secular world and a Christian church.

Student ministry is the first entry point. There are many Inderican students in professional and non-professional schools, some of whom have never stayed outside the home and are now in a new environment for the first time. Also, there are many Enteran students in schools around America, in a new country and a new environment. A student-focused ministry, especially on college campuses, can influence young minds to the gospel of hope. If the church does not have resources of money or personnel, they can team up with organizations that specifically work on college campuses.

Freedom ministry is another entry point. There are many Indericans who, unbeknownst to their oblivious Enteran parents, are struggling with alcohol, drugs, sex, or other addictive habits. The honor that accompanies the Indian family is such that the family would prefer that no one know about the "prodigal son." Thus, such a family is more likely to seek a freedom ministry in an American Church than in an Indian Church, just so that any honor can be salvaged from the Indian community. If churches do not have any freedom ministry of their own, they can team up with para-church organizations that work among such people.

Small groups are also an entry point. Indians like the fellowship of small groups of people. That is one of the reasons most Indian churches are small churches. A small church feels like a large family. Inviting an Indian family to a small group will be a good entry point. If there are only a few Indians in an American church, those Indians can be part of a small group.

Service is also valued. Many Enterans who arrived from India were pleasantly surprised to see the support and donations that they received from American churches so that they could settle down here. America is a giving country, and Americans give generously. Many countries outside of America, including in India, are not known to be giving. Enterans are taken aback by the sacrificial attitude that Americans exhibit toward any perceived need.

Family programs are another entry point. Parenting seminars, marriage seminars, and any program that encourages the togetherness of a family will be attractive to Indians. This includes any age-appropriate ministry for different members of the family, like summer school for kids, youth meetings, and children's church. Even if a church does not have strong family-based programs, they can work with other para-church organizations to have regular seminars so that Hindus from the society would be invited to the church.

There are many areas in which both the Indian and American churches have failed in their attempts at evangelism among Hindus. However, with a little organized effort, all hope is not lost. There are still many points in the church, which can attract Indians.

Notes:

98 Many of the points in this chapter are from a survey of twenty-six churches in the following states: Illinois, Texas, New York, Pennsylvania, California, Massachusetts, Georgia, and New Jersey. This is a survey that I conducted via the internet. The results are mentioned in the following sections. In 2000 most Indians were found in the following states (in descending order): California, New York, New Jersey, Texas, Illinois, Florida, Pennsylvania, Michigan, Maryland, Virginia, Georgia and Massachusetts; http://www.indianembassy.org/ind_us/census_2000/ia_population_map_2001.pdf (accessed May 7, 2010).

Both the terms Indians and Hindus have been used in this chapter. This is because there are several points that are relevant to Indians in general and other points that are specific to Hindus. Where the terms Indian has been used, it is also applicable to Hindus as well.

99 George, *Understanding the Coconut Generation*, 138.
100 George, *Understanding the Coconut Generation*, 156.
101 George, *Understanding the Coconut Generation*, 142.
102 Thirumalai, *Sharing Your Faith*, 14.
103 George, *Understanding the Coconut Generation*, 157.
104 Thirumalai, *Sharing Your Faith*, 112-113.

Five

The Hindu Concept of Bhakti

WHAT IS *BHAKTI*?

The *Bhakti Marga* is one of the three major ways that Hindus can relate to God. *Bhakti* is the love or devotion of a devotee to a personal god.

As a way of salvation, *Bhakti* made a dramatic entry in the Bhagvad Gita in the 4th century. As a religious movement it grew rapidly under the dynamic initiative of Ramanuja in the 12th century. Since then *Bhakti* has remained a distinct religious feature and perhaps the most influential spiritual factor of Hinduism, rejuvenating and transforming the hearts of numerous adherents of the faith.[105]

Devotional Hinduism (*Bhakti*) grew during the Muslim period of Indian history (1200-1757 CE). This may be related to the growth of Islamic traditions, especially Sufi devotional mysticism. It is hard to say which influenced the other.[106]

NATURE OF THE *BHAKTI* RELATIONSHIP

Bhakti is essentially a mystical, spiritual relationship. God is considered as a person with distinct attributes who indwells the devotee, empowering him or her from within. *Bhakti* also expresses itself emotionally, to the point that the worshipping devotee is so caught up in a deep ecstatic experience that he or she is unaware of the environment. Of course, this is not the rule. There are many times when a devotee is not frenetic during the course of worship. Thirdly, this *Bhakti* relationship is a matter of one's personal *experience* in which the devotee experiences God's love filling his or her heart.

The devotee also experiences a mystical *union* with the object of his devotion. This union is different from the metaphysical union in Advaita philosophy, wherein the *atman* (soul) loses its identity when he merges with the *Brahman* (Ultimate Being). Rather, this union is one of surrender to the love of God and the submission of one's life to the perfect will of God. Finally, this relationship is *exclusive*. The devotee usually has a monotheistic outlook and considers all other gods as illusory. Thus, the devotee chooses one deity and is completely devoted to it. "*Bhakti* is therefore a definite, intense and exclusive spiritual relationship between bhakta and a personal god of his or her worship and love."[107]

THE GOAL OF BHAKTI

The outcome of a person's living in complete devotion to one's god is firstly, personal salvation for the devotee. Since *Bhakti* is one of the three *margas* (ways) by which a person can obtain salvation, *Bhakti* secures the release of the devotee from a painful and fleeting world. This *marga* is the most natural because it does not require the suppression of one's impulses but its siphoning toward God. Secondly, *Bhakti* is for the love of God for God's sake. There are two kinds of *Bhakti* – *saguna* (personal devotion offered to a particular personal god with attributes) and *nirguna* (personal devotion offered to an impersonal god that has no attributes. Saguna *Bhakti* is a lower level *Bhakti* that includes *tamas* (loving god for fulfillment of carnal desires), *rajas* (seeking god for power and fame), and *satvika* (performance of disinterested action for action's sake). The upper level devotion is *nirguna Bhakti*, which loves god for god's sake without any ulterior motive. Finally, the goal of *Bhakti* can be for purely material ends.[108]

BHAKTI IN THE BHAGVAD GITA[109]

The Bhagvad Gita is the most popular scripture in contemporary Hinduism. It is the premier *Bhakti* literature in Hinduism, even though the concept of *Bhakti* was always hidden within the multiple layers of Hinduism. The entire book is one of devotion to Krishna, one of the incarnations of Vishnu. Even so, the latter parts of the Mahabharata (of which the Bhagvad Gita is a part) talk about devotion to Siva.

The main features of the *Bhakti* concept as elucidated by this book are, first, that *Bhakti* is a *way of salvation*. In fact, Krishna says that the *Bhakti Marga* is superior to the earlier *Margas* of Hinduism – *Karma Marga* and *Jnana Marga*. The Bhagvad Gita says:

(9) My dear Arjuna, O winner of wealth, if you cannot fix your mind upon Me without deviation, then follow the regulated principles of *Bhakti-*yoga. In this way you will develop a desire to attain to Me. (10) If you cannot practice the regulations of *Bhakti*-yoga, then just try to work for Me, because by working for Me you will come to the perfect stage. (11) If, however, you are unable to work in this consciousness, then try to act giving up all results of your work and try to be self-situated. (12) If you cannot take to this practice, then engage yourself in the cultivation of knowledge. Better than knowledge, however, is meditation, and better than meditation is renunciation of the fruits of action, for by such renunciation one can attain peace of mind.[110]

Salvation by this method is open to all and can never be lost.[111]

Second, *Bhakti* is about *love*. The Gita talks about four kinds of worshippers – the *avta*, the penitent one; the *jijnasu*, the seeker of knowledge; the *artharthin*, the desirer of wealth; the *jnanin*, the man of vision. The vision is that vision of the devotee to be one with Krishna. Of course, this oneness is not like the monistic metaphysical oneness the *Jnana marga* in the Upanishads talks about. This is a moral oneness. Krishna says that a person with that vision is the perfect devotee.

Third, *Bhakti* is *self-surrender*. This is not the losing of oneself seen in *Jnana Marga*, but the voluntary submission of oneself to God without losing one's identity. Krishna demands an undivided and unwavering surrender from his devotees.[112]

DISTINCT FEATURES OF BHAKTAS[113]

When looking at the key characteristics of Hindus throughout the ages, the features of those who follow the *Bhakti marga* are unique. Firstly, they have a passion to know God and to have fellowship with him. They are never content with mechanical, mindless action without the passionate experience of being with God. Secondly, they have a different view of salvation. Hinduism generally believes that salvation is either going to heaven or just an escape from the bondage of *karma*. *Bhaktas* go even further. For them, devotion to God is not the means to salvation; it is the end in itself. Their sole aim is to be in close communion with God and experience his presence. Thus, their view of salvation is a higher view. Thirdly, *bhaktas* have a desire for fellowship with other believers. In stark contrast to other factions of Hinduism that seek to get away from the bustle of life to spend time alone with God, *bhaktas* desire to fellowship with other *bhaktas*. This desire is so powerful that it transcends even the centuries-old barriers of the caste system.

CORRELATION TO EVANGELISM

Martin Alphonse makes a strong case that the concept of *Bhakti* was inherent within Hindu scriptures from the very beginning and was the crux of the Hindu experience. Thus, this is the most important unifying theme in Hinduism, with all its varied segregations, and these *bhaktas* are the unifying faction in Hindu society. It follows then that any evangelism that is focused on *bhaktas* will have widespread implications. In order to keep the gospel thus focused on *bhaktas,* the gospel needs to be contextualized to the Hindu bhaktas who are perhaps nearer in their response to the gospel more than any other type of Hindu. They are markedly different from all the other types of Hindus, for they are keenly spiritual minded, show enormous interest in spiritual issues and are willing to listen to spiritual conversations. Above all they are a very influential people within Hinduism, and quite contagious in spreading fast and with passion whatever they have found to be true in their experience.[114]

Indian Christians have usually responded to *Bhakti* in a variety of ways. They have expressed a desire to learn from Hindu *Bhakti*. The main reason for this thinking is to contextualize the gospel of Jesus to the *bhaktas* for the purpose of evangelizing them. They have also developed an apologetic approach to *Bhakti* by making a comparative study between Christianity and Hindu

Bhakti and then defending the Christian faith over *Bhakti*. This is usually done by claiming strong Christian influence on the *Bhakti* movement, claiming that Christianity or Jesus Christ is the fulfillment of Hindu *Bhakti* or that Christianity is the true *Bhakti marga*.[115] In light of the comparisons between Christianity and *Bhakti*, the comparison between the Hindu and Christian concepts of grace is interesting. The similarities are: belief in a personal god, the reverent humility on the part of the devotee, and belief in God's incarnation. The key differences between the two are: the cross of Christ and the person of Christ.[116]

BHAKTI AS PREPARATION FOR EVANGELISM

Bhakti is seen as a preparation for evangelism.[117] There are two ways of looking this concept. Firstly, *Bhakti* is seen as part of God's general revelation of himself in Hinduism. Three evidences are cited to prove this thought. The work of the Holy Spirit is believed to be prevalent in the noble elements of the *Bhakti* tradition. In addition, the *bhakta* has an insatiable longing for God. This desire for God can be so intense that the Hindu is willing to deny some of the fundamental principles of Hinduism in order to get access to a God to worship and have fellowship with. Finally, the Hindu belief in the divine incarnation is part of God's general revelation. This concept is that the preserver God in *Bhakti marga*, Vishnu, comes in ten human incarnations. The tenth incarnation, Kalki, is still to come in the future. This incarnation is to be born of a virgin and is called Nishkalanka or faultless, and will ride a white horse, going throughout the earth to destroy the wicked and usher in the age of righteousness. This seems to be a rendering of the first and second advents of Christ.[118]

Secondly, *Bhakti* is seen as a preparation for evangelism. This is because "the Hindu mind springs almost instinctively to a deep admiration for Christ; his character is more readily understood by easterners than by westerners and there is more natural reverence and devotion among the former than the latter."[119]

Some of the appealing characteristics of Christ are his control over the exercise of power and his unique teachings, especially those that kindle a sense of devotion. The gospel of John is very attractive to the *bhaktas*. However, in spite of this admiration for Christ, it is very difficult for the Hindu to accept the exclusive claims of Christ. Hindus also care much less about the authority of the Bible, the teachings of the Church, or the correctness of the Church's doctrines and creeds. Thus, they are also not interested in Christianity. In a Hindu mind, Christianity is a western religion and, being associated with western culture, Christianity is guilty of immorality by association. Their only attraction is toward Christ. E. Stanley Jones noticed that a large number of Hindus were turning to Christ to fulfill their moral and spiritual cravings.[120]

OBSTACLES TO EVANGELISM AMONG *BHAKTAS*

There are three main reasons why fruit has not been forthcoming in evangelism among *bhaktas*. The first is syncretism. Hindus historically assimilate all foreign beliefs as a part of their own, and it is no different with the Christian faith. This is usually the boast of a Hindu, namely that Hindusim can accommodate any onslaught to it and it is done primarily through syncretism.

The second obstacle is relativism. As a result of the similarities between *Bhakti* and the Christian faith, it is possible for *bhaktas* to reject any attempts of evangelism and defend their beliefs.[121] The third obstacle is the Christian image. The foreign image of Christianity and hence the foreign image of Christ himself is a major barrier to evangelism among devout Hindus.

EVANGELIZATION OF *BHAKTAS*[122]

There has been a tendency among western missionaries to India to consider Hindus as pagans and as living in deep darkness. This is not true. *Bhaktas* are almost in a pre-Christian state. A secular westerner is more pagan than a *bhakta* who is in deep devotion and in spiritual relationship with his or her god. This should be an encouragement for those involved in evangelism among *bhaktas*, that a *bhakta* is not far from the kingdom of God.

The Message

In light of the Hindu attraction to Christ and Christ alone, it becomes clear, then, that the main focus of an attempt at evangelization should be based purely on Christ. It is important not to syncretize the person of Christ to fit into the Indian setting to increase his acceptability. Also, it is important not to "hide" any of his claims. Hindus need to see Christ just the way he is without any watering down or hyperbole of his personality.[123]

The authority and inspiration of the Bible matter little to Hindus. There is difference of opinion, however, about the aspect of Christ's personality that should be emphasized. Some writers believe that the immanence of Christ should take preeminence in the message. Christ is often preached as teacher, preacher, prophet and king, physician and priest, but the Savior that lives among us as Emmanuel is often missed. To a *bhakta*, a God who lives within one's heart is highly appealing.[124] However, it is sensible to start on those issues on which there is agreement, like Christ the perfect man and the perfect teacher, before the claim of Christ to be the only way to the Father. It is not necessary to start on the exclusiveness of Christ and thus stop all further conversation. Paul Sudhakar, a convert from Hinduism says, "No Hindu comes to Christ to accept Christ intellectually that Jesus is the only Saviour, but because he needs Christ."[125]

Other scholars believe that the emphasis should be on Christ as the fulfiller of a *bhakta's* longing. The core need of a *bhakta* is a relationship with a personal god, and it is being filled by Krishna and other gods. This need can be filled completely by Christ. In addition, Christ needs to be presented as one who can fully satisfy the emotional need of the human heart. Since the *bhaktas* have an emotional rather than an intellectual need, in presenting the gospel, the evangelist should not get caught up in an intellectual argument. Thus, there should also not be an emphasis on the concept of sin but on the person of Christ, who fulfills the spiritual need for divine fellowship.

The Attitude

There are usually three attitudes that Christians have when evangelizing Hindus:[126] evangelism seen as a conquest; evangelism seen as academic, in which Hinduism is observed as just another religion; and a syncretistic approach in which the Christian message is conformed to the Hindu context to obtain acceptance. What is needed is an emphatic attitude. To obtain an emphatic attitude to share an experiential gospel to a Hindu, it is essential for the evangelist to have had a deep spiritual experience of the Christ that he or she is preaching about.

Evangelism among *bhaktas* can be favorable and unfavorable at the same time. It is unfavorable because *bhaktas* usually have devotion and love for the one God that they have chosen to worship. They may be hesitant to "try" another God, as opposed to a Hindu who believes in all gods and, therefore, includes Jesus as one of the many gods.

However, a *bhakta* Hindu is the closest to a Christian in spiritual outlook and spiritual experience of any of the kinds of Hindus. Thus, a mere change in the object of devotion can lead to conversion. Methods of evangelism that show forth the unedited nature of Christ will exhibit the superiority of Jesus among other gods.

Notes:

105   Martin Paul Alphonse, "The Gospel and Hindu '*Bhakti*': Indian Christian Responses from 1900 to 1985 – A Study in Contextual Communication" (PhD diss., Fuller Theological Seminary, School of World Mission, 1990), 83.
106   Larson, "Hinduism in India," 191.
107   Alphonse, "The Gospel and Hindu '*Bhakti*", 75-79.
108   Alphonse, "The Gospel and Hindu '*Bhakti*," 79-82.
109   Ibid., 92-95.
110   A.C. *Bhakti*vedanta Swami Prabhupada, *Bhagvad Gita* 12.9-12, http://www.asitis.com/12/ (accessed December 5, 2009).
111   *Bhagvad Gita*, 9.26-31.
112   *Bhagvad Gita*, 9.34, 18.65-66.
113   Alphonse, "The Gospel and Hindu '*Bhakti*,'" 114-117.
114   Alphonse, "The Gospel and Hindu '*Bhakti*,'" 113.
115   Alphonse, "The Gospel and Hindu '*Bhakti*,'" 119-136.
116   Sabapathy Kulandran, *Grace: A Comparative Study of the Doctrine in Christianity and Hinduism* (London: Lutterworth Press, 1964), 241, quoted in Alphonse, "The Gospel and Hindu '*Bhakti*,'" 133-134.
117   Alphonse, "The Gospel and Hindu '*Bhakti*,'" 149-162.
118   J. Takle, "How Should We Missionaries Present Christ?" *Harvest Field* 12 (1901): 28, quoted in Alphonse, "The Gospel and Hindu '*Bhakti*,'" 157.
119   Pakenham Walsh, "The Attitude of the Educated Hindu Mind toward Christianity," *Harvest Field* 17 (1906): 226 in Alphonse, "The Gospel and Hindu '*Bhakti*,'" 159.
120   Alphonse, "The Gospel and Hindu '*Bhakti*,'" 161.
121   Alphonse, "The Gospel and Hindu '*Bhakti*,'" 300-302.
122   Alphonse, "The Gospel and Hindu '*Bhakti*,'"162-173.
123   W. H. Thorp, "Indigenous Christianity," *Harvest Field* 14, no. 11 (1912), in Alphonse, "The Gospel and Hindu '*Bhakti*,'" 165.

124 Takle, "How Should We Missionaries Present Christ?" 25. in Alphonse, "The Gospel and Hindu '*Bhakti*,'" 163-164.

125 Paul Sudhakar, "How to Prepare the Church for Dialogue," *Religion and Society* 26, no. 1 (1979): 36-41, quoted in Alphonse, "The Gospel and Hindu '*Bhakti*,'" 166-167.

126 Murray C. Rogers, "Hindu and Christian – A Moment Breaks," *Religion and Society* 12, no.1, (1965): 37-38, in Alphonse, "The Gospel and Hindu '*Bhakti*,'" 171.

Part Two

The Theory of Evangelism

Six

Theological Foundations of Evangelism and Correlation to Indian Ministry

JESUS CHRIST

JESUS AS THE CENTER OF EVANGELISM

If there is one theme that is the pivot of the Bible, around which all of Scripture and all of history moves, it would be the person of Jesus Christ. The Old Testament anticipates Him, and the New Testament rejoices in Him. The task of the Church now and the hope for the future all rest in Jesus Christ. The gospel is Jesus himself. The story of the gospel is a narration of the life, death, and resurrection of Jesus as the action of God that both reveals God's passion for the world and achieves God's purpose for that world. The churches of the New Testament preached Jesus as the Christ because of his death and resurrection. Their gospel was about Jesus.[127] Thus, Jesus is the center of evangelism. Guder says, "We are persuaded that any responsible missional ecclesiology must be centered on the hope, the message and the demonstration of the inbreaking reign of God in Jesus Christ."[128]

The Bible is clear on the issue: "That if you confess with your mouth Jesus *as* Lord, and believe in your heart that God raised Him from the dead, you will be saved.... For there is no distinction between Jew and Greek; for the same *Lord* is Lord of all, abounding in riches for all who call on Him; for

'Whoever will call on the name of the Lord will be saved'" (Romans 10:9, 12-13 NASB).

The institution or organism, flawed as it is, that speaks about the reign of Christ, is the Church. The primary mode by which God accomplishes his missional purpose is through the Church. Thus, it is God's intention that the church be closely connected to the vine, Jesus Christ. "The church bears a marked resemblance to the incarnation of Jesus, who, being God was equally real human flesh and life. It is no accident that the church is called the "body of Christ."[129]

Any effort that arises out of the Church and any mission that the Church initiates should have at its core the person and work of Jesus Christ. The body of Christ cannot possibly be involved in anything that excludes the head. Thus any mission is understood as being derived from the very nature of God. It is thus put in the context of the doctrine of the trinity, not of ecclesiology or soteriology. The classical doctrine of the *missio dei* as God the Father sending the Son, and God the Father and the Son sending the Spirit is expanded to include yet another "movement": the Father, Son and Holy Spirit sending the church into the world.[130]

The mission of the church that is based on Christ will fulfill the perfect will of God and will produce long-term fruit. Unfortunately, in a capitalistic market and performance-driven society, it is easy to be sidetracked by church growth principles and strategies. "In our time in history, we talk with an incredible sense of insight about church growth as if we know where the Spirit's coming from and where it is going. The truth of the matter is that any strategy for growth that isn't based on an intimate relationship with Jesus Christ will not prevail in the long run."[131]

HINDU VIEW OF JESUS CHRIST

Christianity is considered by most Hindus to be a western religion, and, hence, Jesus is considered to be a foreign god. It is only the historically acute mind that understands that the gospel arrived in India well before it went to the West. In spite of this general barrier, Hindus have some strong impressions of Jesus.

Avatar (Incarnation)

Hinduism believes that God was incarnated as a human being several times in history. These incarnations took place "whenever and wherever there is a decline in religious practice (*dharmasya*) ... and a predominant rise of irreligion (*adharmasya*)."[132]

Jesus is seen as one of the incarnations of God, and thus he was above the travails of regular humans. Jesus was fully conscious of his mission as an incarnation and clearly understood the objective of his life and the method that he and his followers must use, whether or not the world accepted his message at that time. He knew that it was bound to be accepted eventually. There was no faltering in his consciousness. He definitely expressed the ideal and left the world cheerfully like a great hero.[133]

As an incarnation, Jesus showed the presence of God, led a life that demonstrated how humans are supposed to live, and showed the people the way to be aware of God and to get directly to him. His desire was to "establish a spirit of religion and rescue the souls of men from utter degradation .... give a new spirit and power to the existing real religious attitude."[134]

At the end of his life, Hindus believe, it did not seem that he had fulfilled his purpose since he did not establish the kingdom of God as he wanted. In spite of the initial lack of response from people, Jesus still continued to show love and grace, even to Judas.[135] He was able to transform any person instantaneously and lift him to the presence of God.

Hindus scarcely distinguish between the human and the divine. That Jesus Christ was divine is not a disputable question for many Hindus. However, they find it difficult to believe that Jesus Christ is the only incarnation of the Divine. Jesus is just one among many Prophets or Incarnations.

Mahatma Gandhi also could not bring himself to believe that Jesus was the only way to God:

It was more than I could believe that Jesus was the only incarnate son of God, and that only he who believed in him would have everlasting life.... .my reason was not ready to believe literally that Jesus by his death and by his blood redeemed the sins of the world.... I could accept Jesus as a martyr, an embodiment of sacrifice and a divine teacher but not as the most perfect man ever born. His death on the cross was a great example to the world, but that there was anything like a mysterious or miraculous virtue in it, my heart could not accept.[136]

Oriental[137]

Jesus embodies the ideals of the thoughts and actions of the Eastern world more than the Western world. This is because Oriental people have a theocentric culture compared to western occidental civilization, which is geocentric. Thus, the emphasis of Christ on spiritual life was different from his contemporaries in the Greek and Roman civilizations.

Swami Akhilananda suggests that Jesus and his devotees prescribed different kinds of mystical practices and spiritual exercises. Jesus focused mainly on the kingdom of God and the realization of God, and practiced his religion in prayer and in the application of spiritual ideals in everyday life.[138]

Yogi[139]

This is seen in the context of the *Margas* (Ways) of Hinduism. In *Jnana Marga*, a person performs meditation or yoga to experience oneness with the Ultimate. Jesus is seen as a person who was able, through meditation and prayer, to be united with God. The goal of Hindu dharma is self-realization, and Jesus Christ is the supreme example of this "soul which is totally illumined." The ultimate liberating experience in Hinduism is described as *aham brahma asmi,* i.e. the realization that I am That (Absolute). Only Jesus Christ, according to Hindus, is capable of identifying that Truth with Himself. ("I and the Father are one" [John 10:30]). As a result of his yoga, Jesus was able to get rid of all desires so that he could say, "For where your treasure is, there will your heart be also" (Matt 6:21). The incident of the transfiguration is seen as an example of the divine-human unity Jesus obtained through meditation.

Secondly, a yogi is said to influence and transform people. The Bible is replete with incidents of Christ's influencing power. Thirdly, Jesus is also seen following *Karma Marga*. The example cited in this case is his service during the Last Supper in the upper room when Jesus washed the feet of his disciples. Finally, Jesus is seen following *Bhakti Marga* because of his innumerable statements about love – both to God and to fellow man.

Guru (Teacher)

For many Hindus, Jesus Christ remains an inspiration for social teaching. Mahatma Gandhi found the whole social teaching of Jesus Christ beautifully summarized in the Beatitudes. Gandhi was fascinated by the message of the Gospel or the thought of the preaching of Christ. He said,

I can say that the historical Jesus never interested me. Nothing would change for me if someone proved that Jesus never lived and that the Gospel narration was a fictitious story because the message of the Sermon on the Mount would always remain true for me....During many years of my life I considered Jesus of Nazareth a great Master, perhaps the strongest the world has ever known.... I can say that Jesus holds a special place in my heart as a teacher who has exerted a considerable influence on my life.[140]

However, it could not be said to be a commitment of faith in Christ. Jesus Christ remains for Hindus like Gandhi a supreme human model to be imitated or an inspiration to be referred to.

Superhuman or God

Jesus is considered to be an example of a mature and evolved humanity. Thus, Jesus Christ is not an individual person but a symbol of progressively evolved humanity, or it is a humanity realized in its full manner. Such a view completely de-historicizes Jesus, reducing Him to an illusion. Dr. Sarvapalli Radhakrishnan typifies this attitude: "Every event in the life of Christ, because he is born of the Spirit, is to be seen as a universal-symbolic stage of spiritual life; Christhood is the state of glorious interior illumination in which divine wisdom has become heritage of the soul."[141]

Finally, Hindus consider Jesus as God. Swami Vivekandanda, the person who introduced Hinduism to America, said about Christ, "If I, as an oriental, have to worship Jesus of Nazareth, there is only one way left to me, that is to worship him as god and nothing else."[142] He is not considered as the only God, but as one of the innumerable gods of Hinduism.

KINGDOM OF GOD

The gospel that the apostles preached was about Jesus and was also the central message that Jesus preached. The message that Jesus preached was about the coming reign of God. "Repent for the kingdom of God is at hand" (Mark 1:15).

The central aspect of the teaching of Jesus was that concerning the Kingdom of God. Of this there can be no doubt.... Jesus appeared as one who proclaimed the kingdom; all else in his message and ministry serves a function in relation to that proclamation and derives its meaning from it. The challenge to discipleship, the ethical teaching the disputes about oral tradition or ceremonial law, even the pronouncement of forgiveness of sins and the welcoming of the outcast in the name of God – all these are to be understood in the context of the Kingdom proclamation or they are not to be understood at all.[143]

It was about the Kingdom that Jesus asked the disciples to preach.[144] This would also be the mission of the Church[145] and a central concept of the preaching of the early missionaries.[146]

The Reign of God or the Kingdom of God is a concept that is not completely and clearly defined in Scripture. Jesus chose to explain it in multiple parables. The Kingdom of God is described in several different ways, and one is able to understand bits and pieces of the whole concept. The Church itself was within the overarching boundaries of the Kingdom of God. The Church was not equivalent to the Kingdom, but was a part of it – a significant, nonetheless small, part of it.

There are two important aspects of Jesus' teaching regarding the reign of God.[147] God's reign is not understood as exclusively in the future but as both future and already present. "The kingdom of God is within you" (Luke 17:21). Paradoxically, even though it has already arrived, it is still to come:

"Your kingdom come" (Matthew 6:10). The second aspect is that the ministry of Jesus, presumably characteristic of his Kingdom ministry, launches an all-out attack on evil and the various manifestations of it. Wherever Jesus overcomes evil, there the reign of God comes. It is seen especially in his healings and exorcisms (Luke 11:20; Matthew 12:28).

Paul states the character of the reign of God as being enabled by the Holy Spirit.[148]

The reign of God most certainly arises as God's mission to reconcile the creation accomplished in the death and resurrection of Jesus.... Ruling by way of a cross and resurrection, God thwarts the powers of sin and death that distort the creation once good at its beginning. The future rule of God breaks ahead in time as a harbinger of the world's future to be fully and finally reconciled to God.[149]

Thus, living under the reign of God now is bringing the future forward – living now, as God intends us to live in the future to come. When Jesus said that the Kingdom of God is near, he meant that what was in the future and what was far away is now brought near us and God invites us to enter that life.

The Church is usually seen as an entity that builds and extends the Kingdom of God, but the New Testament does not mention the words *build* and *extend* when talking about the Kingdom. Instead the Bible talks about the Kingdom of God as a gift that one receives. This gift has been given by God for each person to appropriate it (Luke 12:32, Luke 6:20, Mark 10:14). It is also described as something to be inherited.[150] Secondly, the kingdom is seen as a realm that one enters, and thus one is described as being in the Kingdom (Matthew 5:19; 25:21,23; 7:21; Colossians 1:13; 2 Peter 1:11). The Kingdom of God, then, is a gift and a welcome. It is possible to reject that gift and to spurn that welcome, thus rejecting the reign of God.[151]

Jesus equates the Kingdom of God and Life and the Kingdom of God and the Way (Mark 9:45, 47; Acts 19:8-9). In addition, He himself claims to be the Life and the Way. Jesus, then, is the personification of the Kingdom of God; receiving and entering the Kingdom of God is equivalent to receiving the "indescribable gift" of Jesus and entering into a personal relationship with him. Indeed, Jesus has called every person into a personal relationship with him.

RELATIONSHIP BETWEEN THE CHURCH AND THE KINGDOM OF GOD

The notion of the Church has changed from being a place where Christians gather and where the Christian culture is propagated to a body of people that is sent on a mission, thus emphasizing the missional calling of the Church. This difference is important because it underscores the role of the Church in the grand scheme of God. In the first instance, the Church was seen as the place from which missions progressed to the far corners of the world. Now, the Church itself is seen as part of the whole missional plan of God and has been sent out. Mission is thus theocentric instead of ecclesiocentric. Mission is not something that the Church does; rather, mission is something that the Church is a part of.[152] It is imperative to realize the difference between the Church and the Kingdom of God in order to clearly understand the extent and the limits of the role of the Church in the ultimate purpose of God.

The Church has been "called and sent to represent the reign of God."[153] The Church has been sent the same way that Jesus was sent to the earth – to proclaim the gospel. The Gospel of John portrays the missional concept of sending: Jesus was sent by God, Jesus will send the Holy Spirit, Jesus sends the disciples into the world (John 17:8, 16:7, 17:18). The gospel Jesus proclaimed was about the proximity of the Kingdom of God.[154] Since the Church has been sent into the world just as Christ was sent, the same gospel message that Christ preached needs to be preached.[155]

It is imperative that the Church see itself only as a foretaste of the life in the Kingdom of God. God adds to the Church those who are being moved by the work of the Kingdom of God. Indeed, the work that God does cannot be confined only in the Church. The invisible, long arms of the kingdom extend far beyond the visible reaches of the Church. The story of Cornelius in Acts 10 is a case in point. He was not a part of any church, yet God was doing his work in him. It was only in the later stages in the process of conversion that the church was instrumental in the life of Cornelius. God is doing his work beyond the limits of the Church. This is a very important point that changes the way Christians view those outside the Church. No one needs to be in the Church for the process of conversion to start. Since God is at work all the time, He is at work in the lives of many people outside the Church, unbeknownst to the Church. Of course, the Church is used by God to help start the conversion of a wide gamut of people, but there are a lot of people outside the confines of church, some probably in opposition to the church, who are being slowly but surely worked upon by the sovereign Lord. This helps Christians to be more welcoming to those who come through the church doors as those who might be well on their way toward God. It also helps Christians to be less judgmental of those outside the church and those who follow other religions. God may still be working through those religions and their teachings to finally reveal Jesus to its adherents. When Paul preached to the Gentiles at Lystra, he claimed that God has not left himself without witness among a non-Jewish, areligious people. This is true of God's work among all the peoples of the world.

God is at work long before the evangelist starts to work. The Christian's responsibility is merely to keep up with what He is doing in the world. The Church is the agent and the representative of the reign of God.[156] The Church represents the kingdom of God as its community, its servant, and its messenger.[157] It is a unique community that lives under the reign of God, is involved in the world as salt and light, and proclaims to the world the kingdom of God.

CORRELATION IN INDIAN EVANGELISM

In light of the Kingdom concept, evangelism takes a whole different meaning. The mission needs to start in the Church, and the Church needs to monitor itself carefully to see if it is perpetually living in the center of the reign of God. Mission is not seen as flowing from the churched to the unchurched. Instead, everybody is a part of and experiencing the benefits of the Kingdom.

Thus, a Hindu does not need to be in a church to start to hear the gospel message. God may have been working in his or her heart long before any contact with a church. The approach of a Christian toward a Hindu is not "you are a pagan," as has been the attitude for many centuries, but as a people within whom God has already begun his work. It is true that, eventually, every person needs to come into contact with a church to experience the foretaste, fellowship, and the life of the Kingdom of God. However, every person can start at any point, even outside the Church, and continue towards the living God. Thus, the Christian journeys with a joyful and humble attitude, as a co-pilgrim.

PILGRIMAGE

The Church is viewed as the people of God and by inference, a pilgrim church. The biblical model is that of the Moses-led Israelites wandering in the desert. This theme is seen vividly in the book of Hebrews, where Christians are sojourners in a foreign land. The Christian faith, when seen as a pilgrimage, has as its final destination the reign of God, of which the pilgrims have a foretaste here and now. It is toward that fulfillment of the reign of God that every Christian journeys. In this journey toward the reign of God, "God's pilgrim people need only two things: support for the road, and a destination at the end of it. It has no fixed abode here; it is a *paroikia*, a temporary residence. It is permanently underway, toward the ends of the world and the end of time.[158]

EVANGELISM AS A PILGRIMAGE

All people are on a pilgrimage in relation to God. This includes both Christians and non-Christians. No one can really know at what point of that journey anyone is until they are engaged in conversation. Blind categorization of non-believers as lost and in darkness is missing the work of God completely. Since God is at work beyond the Church, he is influencing the lives of people without having to inform the Church of his doings.

God is at work all the time in the lives of people inside and outside the church. He is drawing people toward himself. Thus, there are many stages in a person's journey from the natural man towards a holy God. All people who are on that journey fall in one of these several stages.

1. those who seek the opposite of God
2. those who are indifferent to God
3. those who are certain that there is no God – the Atheist
4. those who doubt the existence of God – the Agnostic
5. those who believe in God, but as an impersonal force – the Deist
6. those who suspect that God might be personal.
7. those who believe in God as personal
8. those who actively seek to know God
9. those who are convinced that God can be known through Jesus.[159]

Thus, different people are at different distances away from a relationship with God. As soon as it is recognized that all people are on a spiritual pilgrimage, no one is really seen as a theistic antagonist, but as a fellow pilgrim in the journey toward God. Thus, the task of the Christian should be to identify and define where a person is on the journey toward God. The Christian needs to discern the questions which must be addressed at such a point, explore those questions in a helpful way, and respond in such a way as to move them toward the next stage in their spiritual journey.

George Hunter revives the centuries-old evangelistic method used by St. Patrick in Ireland, in which point conversion was not practiced. Instead, interested people lived in a common area while they continued in their spiritual journey towards the point of commitment to Christ.[160] This was also how the first century believers looked at evangelism.[161]

It is relevant to note that evangelism among postmoderns is similar to St. Patrick's method, which is what the early church practiced – that it is a pilgrimage and therefore a process. All people who enter a church should be assessed as to the different stages they might be in and then slowly moved to the next stage until everyone reaches the stage of spiritual maturity.

PILGRIMAGE TO AN INDIAN MIND

Pilgrimage is an important part of Hinduism. There are many holy sites scattered throughout India to which millions of Hindus make frequent visits. Hindus believe that the geographic location itself is sacred and is somehow connected to deity. Many of these pilgrimage sites are built with rich religious symbols, giving an aura of holiness so that, when the pilgrim makes his or her way to these places, the pilgrim is able to leave behind the world of society, sin, and nature.[162] What makes that particular location important is the belief that it was the site of some past divine manifestation, that certain deities are more accessible from those specific locations, and if one were to follow the specified guidelines in approach, one would be able to gain access to that deity. Pilgrimage is also done to get goals met, and these goals are specific to the particular deity that is approached. In addition, pilgrimage by itself is seen as meritorious and results in an increase in one's *karma*. The more sacrificial and difficult that particular pilgrimage is made to be results in additional merit.[163]

Pilgrimage is important not only for the obvious reasons "but also because important notions of Hindu theology, philosophy and eschatology are enacted through pilgrim practice."[164] Thus, taking pilgrimage as an allegory of the journey of the soul to God provides a reasonable explanation for the frequent association of pilgrimage and death in the Hindu tradition. Important places of pilgrimage…are celebrated for death related rituals and acts. If the geographical journey to the abode of the deity is taken as an allegory for the passage of the soul through life to God, then the termination of the allegorical journey at the earthly shrine invokes the idea of the completion of the soul's life passage. This … explains why many sacred texts place a value on death in the pilgrimage center (when the reality and the allegory coincide), which guarantees moksa (liberation) for the soul.[165]

Thus, a Hindu is at home with the concept of the soul being on a journey, a life-long journey to God.

CONVERSION

Conversion is a concept at the heart of the Christian faith. Indeed it is at the core of any monotheistic evangelistic religious belief. The Bible indicates what conversion is not (John 1:12): It is not of blood; it is not hereditary, rather a personal, individual unique decision. Conversion is also not "through the will of the flesh"; it is not by personal attempts or striving and by exercise of one's will. Conversion is not by the "will of man" - it needs to come from God, or it is not conversion at all. Conversion is different from proselytism.

Proselytism is a change from one group to another without any necessary change in character and life. It is a change of label, but not of life. Conversion... is a change in character and life followed by an outer change of allegiance corresponding to that inner change.[166]

"Conversion" is made up of "con" – with and "vertere" – to turn, i.e., to turn with. Thus, conversion is not about a person striving to turn to the truth, but of turning with somebody and that somebody is the Holy Spirit. The Holy Spirit works in the subconscious mind and converts the subconscious part of a human being. He cleanses, coordinates, and consecrates the subconscious drives, and so a converted person's reactions then become Christian, since the conscious mind controls actions and the subconscious mind control reactions.[167]

All repentance, conversion, and new birth should be in the context of and towards the kingdom of God (Matthew 4:17; 18:3; John 3:3). Conversion introduces a person into the Kingdom of God and attaches a person to Christ in loyalty and love. Jesus is the gateway into the Kingdom and personifies the Kingdom. Thus conversion is not to an order or an institution or to a movement, or to a set of beliefs, but to a person. Every person is called to belong to Jesus Christ.[168]

Pagan culture prior to Christianity did not have the concept of conversion. The Christian concept of conversion consisted of three parts: belief, behavior, and belonging. It required belief in a Jesus Christ that resulted in a behavioral transformation and a belonging to a community of those who held a similar belief.[169]

TYPES OF CONVERSION
There are two kinds of conversion. The Pauline type of conversion, long thought to be the only way one could be converted, is the first type. In this conversion, the person is instantly and comprehensively transformed. He or she takes a one-hundred-eighty-degree turn and walks toward God. This

person instantly stops the old (bad) habits and never returns to them again. The conversion on the Damascus road is the prime scriptural example.

The second type of conversion – experienced by more people but less dramatic and, therefore, less acknowledged or publicized – is the process of gradual or process conversion. There is no one incident that causes the entire change, but, through a series of incidents, over a long period of time, the person is progressively changed, constantly worked on by God until converted. This is the way the disciples of Jesus were converted, as described in the Gospel of Mark.[170] Since process conversion is more widely experienced, it is quickly apparent that many currently unconverted people probably are at different stages of conversion. A non-Christian can be in one of the following stages of conversion.

1. non-committed
2. committed to Christian ideas
3. committed to Christian ethics
4. committed to Christian community
5. committed to people because of Christ's teaching
6. committed to Jesus and as a result
7. undergo spiritual formation[171]

From a postmodern perspective, conversion involves a change in one's social identity. This change is accomplished by the acquisition of new language skills. Finally, conversion is a paradigm shift in which one looks at the world in a whole different way. The total process of conversion of a postmodern individual takes place in community.[172]

All Christian conversion is based finally on a person's response to Jesus. All other avenues merely lead up to this one final point. A positive response to Jesus, i.e. conversion, should result in life transformation.

First, their eyes need to be opened…They need to see their true state in relationship to God. Perception is foundational to change. Second, having seen, they must turn. They must turn from the way in which they are walking, which is the way of darkness, the way of Satan. They must turn to the way of light which is the way of God. Third, having seen and turned, they will receive forgiveness and sanctification by faith…..(There is) a seeing and a turning which together result in a transformation.[173]

Transformation does not mean that the converted person is instantly made completely holy. Instead, "conversion…. is a change in belief, but it is more than that; it is a change in attitude, but it is still more; it is a change in direction, but more; at the basis it is a change in 'affection.' The conversion is a conversion of our love."[174]

It is a change in the object of our affection. Whereas the unconverted person directed his or her life with affection for self or for the world, the converted person now has a new object of affection – the Lord Jesus. Perfect holiness does not instantly replace unholiness. Instead the direction of the journey is changed toward holiness.

Conversion is conversion from perversion….(The) urges are still there, an integral part of us, but now they are turned toward new ends, with new motives and a new spirit. Conversion doesn't dehumanize us by transplanting an alien life on the framework of the natural, thus setting up a tension between the natural and the supernatural. The supernatural makes us more natural, converting our urges from the unnatural to the truly natural.[175]

CONNOTATIONS OF CHRISTIAN CONVERSION TO A HINDU MIND

Swami Akhilanada equates conversion to a religious experience in which a person is aware of the existence of God. The Hindu equivalent of conversion is initiation. With initiation, a person can focus the mind on a spiritual ideal. The help of a guru is imperative for the process of initiation. At the time of initiation, the guru awakens spiritual consciousness in the disciple, who commits himself wholly to God and to the guru. Total commitment and self-surrender are necessary and result in an inner transformation. This is the beginning of spiritual life and is regarded as the second or spiritual birth of the individual. It is an experience that changes the outlook and way of life of the convert. There are both rare cases of sudden conversion and frequent process conversions. In fact, gradual conversions were encouraged instead of sudden conversions to avoid any opposite reaction. Teachers who are involved in converting people should be well established in God, acquainted with the scriptures, aware of the need of the disciple. Such a teacher should, of a necessity, be initiated himself (or herself) and should be of the highest spiritual quality. The teacher prepares the student gradually for conversion via spiritual discipline.[176]

Christian conversion presupposes that an individual is in a sinful state. Hinduism does not necessarily believe this. Since Hindus seek God for various reasons, it is possible for Hindus to seek God purely to love and enjoy him. In this case, there is no sin involved.[177]

Conversions based on the emotion and decisions made on the spur of the moment are frowned upon because they hold no lasting value. Hence, systematic spiritual practices are needed to establish slow and meaningful conversion. Christian conversions are seen often as emotionally charged. Since many Christian preachers preach about the grace of God, they deemphasize spiritual practices, and thus sudden conversions are not sustained.[178]

The inclusiveness of Hindu thought historically eschewed the necessity for conversion. If there was any opposing opinion or doctrine, it was merely accepted as just another way to reach God. Rabindranath Tagore, Indian poet and philosopher, said that he loved Mark 10:15[179] but left out the issue of conversion seen in Matthew 18:3.[180] He did not like conversion, confusing it with proselytism.[181] However, in recent Indian history, because of the conversion of many Hindus to Christianity and since it was not possible for Hinduism to accept the exclusive Christian claim of access to God, re-conversion of lower caste new Christians back to Hinduism has been attempted.

APPLICATION OF CONVERSION IN THE EXPECTATION OF MINISTRY

Many Hindus were deeply influenced by the moral and spiritual supremacy of Jesus. They had many accusations against the Church and western Christendom but have no objection to Christ. These Hindus do not leave their religion to join a Church, but there is a movement in their minds toward Christ. E. Stanley Jones says that this is not a preparation for conversion or a half conversion, but a conversion in progress. This small start to conversion of the mind toward Christ should be nurtured and developed to a full conversion.[182] They are on the road to conversion.

Not knowing about gradual, progressive conversion causes evangelists to imagine that they have just one chance at sharing the gospel. Many times this "one chance" is used to ram the gospel down an unsuspecting person's throat, without waiting for God to move first. Since most conversion is gradual and ongoing, those who have single, isolated contacts with non-Christian people are unlikely to see the full cycle of conversion. In addition, knowing that different people are in the process of conversion brings patience and hope for the evangelist, even as he or she waits for the final commitment to Jesus Christ.

Jones, a missionary among Hindus for many years, has given some pointers on how to help others into conversion. He claims that anyone who really desires to win others to conversion can do so. Everyone is made for conversion, and the Holy Spirit acts in a person to prepare one for it. Thus, one needs to approach a person with the expectation of winning him or her and not be inhibited by one's own unworthiness since one is not asking for the person to follow him or her, but Christ. There may be an initial resistance, but every person ultimately wants to share his or her inmost longings – the deepest desires of the heart. The goal of evangelism should be the surrender of the self, not a surrender to different, other peripheral issues, hence the pressing need to get to the root of the issue as soon as it is possible. The root of the issue is the lack of surrender of the self; thus, conversion is about getting to that issue and not being sidetracked by the surrender of peripheral things. Once converted, the focus should be to connect immediately to a church fellowship for long term growth.[183]

CONCLUSION

The essence of the Kingdom of God is the person of Jesus Christ. He is the "gift" that the people of the kingdom receive. With him the people of the kingdom enter into a relationship. That is why it is essential to keep Jesus as the centerpiece of evangelism. All church growth principles and strategies should keep the focus on Jesus Christ. Every person is thus on a journey in relation to him. Some people are headed away from him and some others are going toward him. Conversion is necessary to begin this pilgrimage toward him, as well as being necessary at every stage of that pilgrimage.

This unchanging core of evangelism is not dependent on culture, people, language, and age. This was true during the time of Jesus, during the premodern era, and during the modern era. Even in the relativistic outlook of the postmodern era, this core will be unchanging and true.

Notes:

127 Guder, ed., *Missional Church*, 87-88.

128 Guder, ed., *Missional Church*, 10.

129 Guder, ed., *Missional Church,*, 13.

130 David Bosch, *Transforming Mission: Paradigm Shifts in Theology of Mission* (Maryknoll, NY: Orbis, 1991), 390.

131 Erwin McManus, quoted by Robert E. Webber, *The Younger Evangelicals* (Grand Rapids, MI: Baker Books, 2002), 121.

132 Prabhupada, *Bhagavad Gita* 4.7.

133 Swami Akhilananda, "Hindu view of Christ" in *Christianity: Some Non-Christian Appraisals*, ed. David W. McKain (New York: McGraw-Hill Book Company, 1964), 36.

134 Akhilananda, "Hindu view of Christ", 47-48.

135 Akhilananda, "Hindu view of Christ", 49-50.

136 C. Manshardt, ed., *The Mahatma and the Mission* (Navajivan, India: Navajivan Trust, 1941), quoted in *Christianity*, ed. McKain, 75.

137 Akhilananda, *Hindu View of Christ* (New York: Philosophical Library, 1949), 45-71.

138 Some of the references given to support the view that he is oriental in His outlook: Matthew 6:24,25,28,29,32,33.

139 Akhilananda, *Hindu View of Christ,* 72-99.

140 Felix Machado, "How Do Hindus View Jesus Christ?" *The Examiner*, October 10, 1998, http://www.hvk.org/articles/1098/0053.html (accessed December 7, 2009).

141 Machado, "How Do Hindus View Jesus Christ?"

142 Swami Vivekandanda, *The Complete Works of Swami Vivekandanda* (Mimora, Himalyalas: Advaita Ashrama, Mayavah, 1931), 134, quoted in Akhilananda, *Hindu View of Christ*, 55.

143 Norman Perrin, Rediscovering the Teaching of Jesus (New York: Harper & Row, 1967), 54, quoted in *Missional Church*, ed. Guder, 89.

144 Matthew 10:7 – "As you go, preach this message: 'The kingdom of heaven is near'" (NIV).

145 Matthew 24:14 – "And this gospel of the kingdom will be preached in the whole world as a testimony to all nations, and then the end will come" (NIV).

146 This is found in Acts 8:12; 14:21; 19:8; 20:25; 28:23; 28:31.

147 Bosch, *Transforming Mission*, 32-33.

148 Romans 14:17 – "For the Kingdom of God is not a matter of eating and drinking, but of righteousness, peace and joy in the Holy Spirit" (NIV).

149 George R. Hunsberger, "Missional Vocation," in *Missional Church*, ed. Guder, 91.

150 This can be seen in Matthew 25:34; James 2.5; Matthew 5:5; 1 Corinthians 6:9-10, 15:50; Galatians 5:20; Ephesians 5:5.

151 Guder, ed., *Missional Church*, 93-97.

152 Guder, ed., *Missional Church*, 79-83.

153 Hunsberger, "Missional Vocation," *Missional Church*, ed. Guder, 77.

154 Mark 1:14 - 15 After John was put in prison, Jesus went into Galilee, proclaiming the good news of God. "The time has come," He said. "The Kingdom of God is near. Repent and believe the good news!"

155 John 17:18 - "As you sent me into the world, I have sent them into the world."

156 This can be seen in Matthew 16:19, John 20:19-23; Colossians 4:11; and 2 Corinthians 5:20.

157 This triad seen in Scripture was highlighted by Hans Hoekendijk and Hendrik Kraemer in the 1950s and by the WCC in 1961, in *Missional Church*, ed. Guder, 102-109.

158 Bosch, *Transforming Mission*, 374.

159 Richard Peace, "Re-inventing Evangelism" (lecture, School of Theology, Fuller Theological Seminary, April 11-22, 2005).

160 George Hunter, *The Celtic Way of Evangelism* (Nashville, TN: Abingdon Press, 2000).

161 Michael Green, *Evangelism in the Early Church* (Grand Rapids, MI: Eerdmans Publishing Company, 1970).

162 E. Alan Morinis, *Pilgrimage in the Hindu Tradition* (New Delhi: Oxford University Press, 1984), 279.

163 Morinis, *Pilgrimage in the Hindu Tradition*, 279-282.

164 Morinis, *Pilgrimage in the Hindu Tradition*, 283-284.

165 Morinis, *Pilgrimage in the Hindu Tradition*, 297.

166 Jones, *Conversion*, 16.

167 Jones, *Conversion*, 230-236.

168 Jones, *Conversion*, 243-244.

169 Green, *Evangelism in the Early Church*, 144-147.

170 Richard V. Peace, *Conversion in the New Testament, Paul and the Twelve* (Grand Rapids, MI: Eerdmans Publishing Co., 1999). Peace contends that Mark sequences the process of the conversion of the disciples as they went through six different revelations: Jesus the Teacher, Jesus the Prophet, Jesus the Messiah, Jesus the Son of Man, Jesus the Son of David, Jesus the Son of God.

171 Peace, "Re-inventing Evangelism."

172 Brad J. Kallenberg, *Live to Tell: Evangelism in a Postmodern World* (Grand Rapids, MI: Brazos Press, 2002), 31-46.

173 Peace, *Conversion in the New Testament*, 25.

174 Peace, *Conversion in the New Testament*, 46.

175 Peace, *Conversion in the New Testament*, 43.

176 Akhilananda, *Hindu View of Christ*, 252-256.

177 Akhilananda, *Hindu View of Christ*, 251.

178 Akhilananda, *Hindu View of Christ*, 256-257.

179 "Truly I say to you, whoever does not receive the kingdom of God like a child will not enter it at all" (Mark 10:15 NASB).

180 "Truly I say to you, unless you are converted and become like children, you will not enter the kingdom of heaven" (Matthew18:3 NASB).

181 Jones, *Conversion*, 40.

182 Jones, *Conversion*, 95.

183 Jones, *Conversion*, 218-225.

Seven

Postmodernism

The context of ministry is changing. In addition to the geometric progression of technology and the differences in generations comes an added influence—the end of the centuries-old way of life and the largely untried conglomeration of postmodernism. Postmodernism as a context for life is a recent development. Since it is an important development, an understanding of its features and the adaptation of evangelism to its adherents is warranted.

IMPORTANT FEATURES OF POSTMODERNISM

The modern era began at the Renaissance and coalesced at the Enlightenment. René Descartes laid the philosophical foundation with his focus on doubt. For him, the only indubitable fact was a thinking human. Isaac Newton then gave the scientific basis for the modern view by picturing the physical world as a machine with laws and rules that can be discerned by the human mind.[184]

KNOWLEDGE

Modernity elevates the position of humans in the universe and assumes that everything can be known. Modernity thus asserts that knowledge is good and can be attained through rationalization. Hence, knowledge is also objective, and anyone without bias or emotion is able to grasp the truth about the different facets of the universe. The modern view thus elevates the individual and emphasizes the autonomous self.

Postmodernism, starting with Nietzsche, rebelled against modernism. Postmodernism claims that knowledge is not inherently good. As far as literary works, postmodernism says these works are an attempt to make sense of senseless human experiences. In the same vein, there is no one meaning to a text. Multiple interpretations are possible based on the person who reads the text. More specifically, interpretations vary based on the community in which a person lives. Thus, knowledge is subjective, not objective. There is no one truth, only multiple interpretations of a view. One should give up the task of searching for the truth and aim to merely continue the conversation. Since there is no one truth, no one is right and no one is wrong. Everybody is just different. Postmodernity also devalues reason as the only determinant of truth, and adds emotion and intuition as alternative paths.[185]

Contrary to modern thinking that humans can know everything and, therefore, master everything, post modernity says that humanity will not be able to solve the problems of mankind and that things need not get better with each passing day. This anti-modern stance of postmodernism in its rejection of the Enlightenment mindset makes for a negative outlook. There is no confidence in human ability. Individualism is seen as the hindrance to human survival. Humans can survive only in community and cooperation; hence, there is opposition to everything that is individualistic.

COMMUNITY

Postmodernity focuses more on community than on individualism. The modern pattern of individualistic existence is held in disdain. On the contrary, each person, though unique, is recognized and identified by community. Postmodernism believes in community on all levels. It believes in integration of human beings and also integration of all the dimensions of each human being. The segregation of humanness and human society into different parts is a modern thought. According to postmodernism, it is in the context of this community of humanity that truth can be understood.

Postmodern truth is relative to the community in which a person participates. And since there are many human communities, there are necessarily different truths. Most postmoderns make the leap of believing that this plurality of truth can exist alongside one another. The postmodern consciousness, therefore, entails a radical kind of relativism and pluralism.[186]

Since the community and belief is so closely linked, the two should of a necessity be concordant. Any sort of discordance between belief and life is interpreted as hypocrisy.

STRUCTURE AND RELATIVITY

Postmodernism is different from modernity in its lack of organized structure. Postmodern lives are not arranged in order. Thus, completely contradictory issues can co-inhabit the same person, and contradictory viewpoints can co-exist in the same community without much ado.

In addition, the postmodern world has brought with it relativism. It is wrong, the world claims, for anyone to assert his or her knowledge of absolute truth. There is no one truth. Each person's beliefs are to be recognized, without having to submit to another viewpoint. Ravi Zacharias says,

One characteristic of postmodern thinking is extreme relativism..... Postmodernism is dangerous not only because of what it has done to the secular person, but also because it destroys our apologetic, our methods for determining truth. What's happening in the West with the emergence of postmodernism is only what has been in much of Asia for centuries but under different banners[187]

EXPERIENCE

There is an increasing movement away from reason to experiences. Each person is unique, and, therefore, each person's experience is unique and valid. Since experiences are predominant, there need not be a rational explanation for anyone's feelings concerning any issue.

The modern era is seen as the industrial age with the factory as its mascot. The postmodern era is seen as the information age with the computer as its mascot. The explosion of information in this age has brought the world closer, blurred the local boundaries, and created a true global village. This information has resulted in an enormous growth of knowledge ironic in the postmodern world that does not believe that all things can be known.

THE POSTMODERN WORLD VIEW[188]

Postmodernism and Knowledge

Postmoderns have no single worldview. They attempt to replace the concept of one worldview with multiple worldviews. In this way, they have replaced knowledge with interpretation.

Firstly, postmodernism is seen as the end of the concept of a single worldview. Modernism is based on the concept that reality is ordered and that it is possible to understand that order by looking at the laws of nature. The Enlightenment is based on comprehending and using these laws for the benefit of mankind. Postmodernism rejects this view of objective knowledge and, therefore, the presence of an objective world. This is because of the postmodern rejection of a realistic understanding in favor of a non-realistic understanding. In modernism, truth is the correspondence between humans' assertions and the objective reality of those assertions. This is called the correspondence theory, in which one is able to verify the correspondence between statements and their validity. This concept is projected further so that the modernist thinks that he can know the entire universe and thus reality and attempts to explain the logical steps in that knowledge. Thus the modernist claims by projection that it is possible for humans to know everything. Postmodernism rejects the concept that the world is established, and people need to find out and can find out everything about it. They believe that the world is not just a collection of physical objects, but, rather, whatever each person brings into it. It is not possible for anybody to know anything outside of his or her sphere of being. Since knowledge is thus based on each individual, it is a subjective view of the world instead of an impersonal objective one. In addition, the recent globalization of the world has thrown many different cultures into relevance so that the western culture is not seen as the gold standard that everyone is striving to be. Postmodernism says that everyone needs to come to terms with the fact that there are multiple cultures and multiple realities, all coexisting together in this giant cauldron while maintaining their individual differences and identities. Thus, it is a pluralistic view of knowledge. Since there is not one objective view of the world or reality, it is possible to have multiple views, even contradictory views, exist side-by-side.

Secondly, Postmodernism is seen as the end of the one grand story. In the pre-modern era, the lives of people were controlled by cultural myths and religious doctrine. Modernity attempted to rationalize the whole world. Thus, they replaced myths and stories to make way for reason and logic. The basis of modernity was that there was one big story and it was possible to understand the whole reality (universe) using science and reason and thus understand the whole story. Postmodernism believes that there are innumerable small stories that do not necessarily need to connect to each other to form one whole. All these small stories and realities can co-exist side by side.

Thirdly, Postmodernism is seen as the end of science. Modern science arose in order to quell the pre-modern myths that drove the lives of people. The purpose of science was to make the whole universe understandable, sensible, and unified. Science counted religious and cultural leaders as its enemies because they were the ones who continued on with the myths and doctrines. Science replaced myths and doctrines, using facts and knowledge. The continued progress of science would lead to consensus and continue to fill in the blanks of the grand picture of reality. Since postmodernism believes that there is no one picture, it follows that that is the end of the scientific road.

Postmodernism and Science
The modern idea of a single universe was lost. Postmodernism does not accept the vision of a single united world.

In connection with this, the postmodern intellectual ethos resists explanations that are held to be all-encompassing and universally valid. Postmoderns are inclined to prize differences over uniformity and to respect the local and particular more than the universal.[189]

It was an intellectual revolution spearheaded by Galileo and consummated by Newton that defined modernity. The scientific enterprise had begun. Science began to quantify and objectify the known and unknown world. Laws, equations, theorems, and formulas gave a mechanical structure to reality. This outlook reduced the universe to particles and the inter-relationship between them. The climax notion of modern science was that all knowledge, the universe, and all reality could be known quantitatively, mechanically and fully. In this context, the very branch of science that set modernity into motion – physics – began to flounder. Increasingly, evidence began to show that the universe is not as mechanical and quantifiable as initially thought. Max Planck said that energy travels in packets (quanta) instead of a constant flow. Einstein said that light is both a wave and a packet of energy (photons). Bohr said that electrons did not have the simplistic trajectory that was initially thought, but jump from orbit to orbit. Louis de Broglie said that all matter has both particle and wave like properties. The birth of this quantum theory signaled the beginning of postmodern science. At the same time, Einstein formulated his theories of general and special relativity. He disproved the absoluteness of space and time. Matter and energy are also not independent but are inversely related as in $E=mc^2$. Also, gravity is a curvature of the space-time continuum.[190] When one sees all these new theories together, it is instantly obvious that there are a great many variables – matter and energy, particle-form and wave-form, space and time, for example. It is impossible, then, to create a single model that can explain the total complexities of the universe. The clear-cut explanation of modern science has been challenged. Heisenberg's uncertainty principle of 1927 basically states that the indeterminacy of all phenomena cannot be overcome by any amount of observation, essentially saying that it is impossible to fully know the universe.[191] Science in this postmodern world is not a compilation of objective universal truths but a collection of research traditions carried by groups of inquirers, and this knowledge is incomprehensible outside of these communities. It is a world which understands itself through biological rather than mechanistic models; a world where people see themselves as belonging to the environment rather than apart from it or over it. A world distrustful of institutions, hierarchies, centralized bureaucracies and male dominated organizations. It is a world where networks and local grassroots activities take precedence over large scale structures and grand designs; a world in which the book age is giving way to the screen age; a world hungry for spirituality yet dismissive of systematized religion. It is a world in which image and reality are so deeply intertwined that it is difficult to draw the line between the two. [192]

The post modern evangelical generation is marked by a post-9/11 era, has recovered the biblical understanding of human nature, is aware of a new context for ministry, stands for the absolutes of the Christian faith in a new way, recognizes that the road to the future runs through the past, is committed to the plight of the poor, especially in urban centers, is willing to live by the rules, increasingly uses technology, is highly visual, communicates through stories, grasps the power of imagination, advocates the resurgence of the arts, appreciates the power of the performative symbol, longs for community, is committed to multicultural communities of faith, is committed to intergenerational ministry, is attracted to absolutes, is ready to commit, searches for shared wisdom, demands authenticity, and realizes the unity between thought and action.[193]

EVANGELISM AND POSTMODERNISM
Evangelicalism was fully developed in the modern context. Thus an important aspect of the Christian message during this era was in the strong defense and apologetic approach. This was done to satisfy the emphasis on scientific proof, enquiry, and rationalization.

POSTMODERNISM AND THE CHRISTIAN FAITH[194]
The postmodern rejection of the correspondence theory undermines the objective claims of truth and, thus, of the gospel. The Christian view is that the God of the Bible is truth and reveals what is truth. The lack of one objective truth precludes anyone from being able to confirm the validity of any interpretation.

The Christian view is also opposed to the postmodern skepticism of the loss of a center. Christianity believes that the center is in Christ Jesus and all things before and after him work in relation to him. Postmodernism rejects the grand story. The modernist rejection of pre-modern myths using rational science has helped to counter many unfounded superstitions. Postmodernism is right in rejecting the modern view that reason can lead to the one story. However, the postmodern rejection of the one-story concept itself is directly opposite to the Christian message. The Christian story is all about the grand narrative of God acting in history and working out everything according to his plan towards one grand climax.

The modern view is that knowledge is certain, objective, and good. The certainty of knowledge rests on the rational nature and capability of man. Knowledge is also completely objective and impersonal. Since knowledge is the basis and the focus of modernism, it is considered to be inherently good. Postmoderism rejects these modern views on knowledge. The Christian view agrees with postmodernism. Rational scientific method is not the only measure of truth. Some parts of truth lie beyond the rational mind. In addition, the fall has corrupted human minds and darkened the understanding (Romans 1:28; Ephesians 4:17; Titus 1:15; 2 Corinthians 4:4; Ephesians 4:18), so to completely depend on one's mind to decipher truth is risky. In addition, knowledge is not completely objective. Humans live in a subjective context, and each person brings to the historical table a part of himself or herself. Man is a part of history as opposed to being a mere spectator and astute student of history. Finally, knowledge is not always good. Having knowledge does not make one a better person. Knowledge is necessary but not necessarily good.

POSTMODERN AND MODERN CHURCHES[195]
In a direct reflection of the modern (boomer generation) and postmodern (generation X) cultures, churches are distinctively different. Boomer churches are highly structured and organized while Xer churches operate with more involvement of the laity. Thus, church staffs are smaller and less hierarchical, and the church is seen to be more theocentric than pastoral-staff-centric.

Baby boomer churches tend to depend heavily on programs, while Xer churches depend more on relationships. Thus, in postmodern churches, all church programs are valued more for the purpose of simply being together than for the purpose of learning. Fellowship trumps content.

Boomer churches emphasize excellence in church ministries while Xer churches emphasize realness. Postmoderns are not overtly concerned with perfection. Instead, they long for genuine spirituality.

Boomer churches call themselves contemporary, while Xer churches have an ancient-future outlook. They are intrigued by Christian tradition and have no qualms of combining the old with the new. Indeed they prefer contemplative, quiet services instead of the bright, loud Boomer services.

Boomer churches are rationalistic, while Xer churches are holistic. Boomer churches attempt to mainly satisfy reason. Xer churches do not focus on just the mind, but give credence to and satisfaction of intellect and emotions, doctrine and intuition.

Boomer churches usually have a competitive streak, while Xer churches are more cooperative. They have less of a "them and us" attitude and more of an "its-all-us" attitude. This stems from Boomer individualism and Xer community orientation.

POSTMODERN CHURCHES AND THE PRE MODERN ERA

The values of the postmodern church reflect in some ways those of the premodern era and not of the modern era.[196]

Return of the "Ecclesial" Paradigm

Postmoderns reject the secularization and the institutionalizing of the Christian faith. They prefer authentic spirituality. Thus, they assert that the church is not a private but a public faith and encourage the living out of one's faith without any dichotomy with the church and outside.

However, postmoderns dislike the large church with its multiple programs. Instead, they prefer smaller churches that are community based, much like a larger family. They are committed to a church that is post-denominational, intercultural, and intergenerational. Boomer churches over time catered to the needs of people not just in the community, but to those outside it as well. This was made possible because of the widespread means for people to commute, even to churches that were further away.

Robert Webber claims that, since the postmodern generation is more community oriented, the need is to rediscover the neighborhood, so that the church is more focused on reaching the neighborhood in which it is located.[197] The modern method of communication was through words and presentations that appealed to the logic and emotions, but, in postmodernity, the goal of evangelism and the medium of evangelism is the community.[198]

The Church Is a People of Ministry

The age where professional vendors of Christian services gave those services to the lay consumers in the church is over. Postmoderns believe that it is not everyone for himself or herself, but everyone for each other. Every believer is seen as a priest and thus in involved in the mission of the church.

It is not about sending out missionaries or even having a mission. Postmoderns are interested in being God's mission. In this respect, they prefer start-up churches instead of traditional, institutionalized churches that need to be changed from the inside out.

POSTMODERNISM AND THE GOSPEL

The gospel of Jesus Christ is above and beyond any culture or era. Indeed, this gospel is able to transform every culture that comes in contact with it. In spite of the apparent discord between the Christian faith and postmodernism, the good news of Jesus Christ is still relevant for a postmodern culture.

A Community Gospel

Modernism elevated the individual above all. Each person was autonomous, and, since reason played a major part, an individual's reason and knowledge gave him or her significance and an identity. The postmodern focuses on the community.

The community is essential in the process of knowing. Individuals come to knowledge only by way of a cognitive framework mediated by the community in which they participate. Similarly, the community of participation is crucial to identity formation.[199]

The Christian view emphasizes the importance of an individual within the community. The individual is important – salvation and judgment is person based, but the individual finds his or her complete meaning within a community. The perfect example is the existence of God as the Trinity. Thus, the gospel needs to be less a verbal presentation and more a continuous, visible reality of life in a community.

An Infinite Gospel
Modernism stressed objective, scientific reason, and so the effective presentation of the gospel was to present reasons as to why Jesus is the only way and why the Christian faith makes logical sense. The gospel in the modern age was defensive and apologetic in an effort to show that science and Scripture are not mutually exclusive.

With the postmodern view going beyond the edges of reason, it is fitting for the presenters of the gospel to show the gospel for what it really is – a gospel that makes sense but at the same time cannot be completely understood, simply because it originated in the infinite mind of God. Thus, a postmodern gospel gives place for mystery and does not attempt to know everything.

A Whole Gospel
Modernism talked about the material and the immaterial parts of humans. The whole business of salvation in the modern context was about salvation of the immaterial, intellectual, and rational part of humans. However, a human is beyond just a mind. The postmodern view gives credence for the whole person in his whole context. Thus the presented gospel should stress on the whole person of a human.

It involves integrating the emotional-affective, as well as the bodily-sensual, with the intellectual-rational within the one human person… our anthropology must take seriously the biblical truth that our identity includes being in relationship to nature, being in relationship with others, being in relationship with God, and, as a consequence being in true relationship with ourselves.[200]

A Wise Gospel

The modern view taught the world to focus on the obtaining and assimilation of knowledge. It focused on human efforts to obtain certain objective and good knowledge. The postmodern focus is on obtaining wisdom. Thus, the gospel should focus on the importance of knowledge and faith. All aspects of life cannot be explained by reason alone. The gospel is beyond pure reason. The emphasis of the gospel should be on the importance of faith on a day-by-day basis in addition to reason.

Robert Webber gives the following approach to evangelism in a post-modern context. First, establish a relationship between a Christian and non-Christian. Then, invite the interested non-Christian to a community where Christians eat, socialize, and discuss spiritual issues. Third, bring the non-Christian to church where the gospel is seen in community and practiced in worship. Fourth, conversion is characterized by believing, behaving, and belonging. Last, conversion is the start, not the end.[201]

POSTMODERNISM TO THE ENTERAN AND INDERICAN

The Enteran generation is modern, while the Inderican generation is post-modern in their outlook. This adds to the differences that exist between the Enteran and the Inderican.

This (Inderican) generation views spirituality from a pluralistic view-point; they are drawn more to the experiential and even mystical experiences rather than rational ones; more open and tolerant view on sexuality; more image driven than words; interactivity in communication; use of creativity etc.[202]

The gap between the two classes gets wider and more complex: Indian-American, Enteran-Inderican, old-young, Boomer-Generation X, and modern-postmodern. Evangelism between the two classes is more sensitive than initially thought. Thus, all the principles of evangelism that relates to modernists apply to Enterans, and all the principles of postmodernists apply to Indericans.

Notes:

184 Stanley J. Grenz, *A Primer on Postmodernism* (Grand Rapids, MI: Eerdmans Publishing Co., 1996), 2-3.

185 Grenz, *A Primer on Postmodernism*, 7.

186 Grenz, *A Primer on Postmodernism*, 14.

187 Ravi Zacharias, "Reaching the 'Happy-Thinking Pagan,'" in *Growing Your Church through Evangelism and Outreach*, 1st ed., Library of Christian Leadership, ed. Marshall Shelley (Nashville, TN: Random House, Inc., 1996).

188 Grenz, *A Primer on Postmodernism*, 39-56.

189 Charles Jencks, "The Postmodern Agenda," in *The Postmodern Reader*, ed. Charles Jencks (New York: St. Martin's Press, 1992), 11, quoted in Grenz, *A Primer on Postmodernism, 49*.

190 Robert Matthews, *Unraveling the Mind of God* (London: Virgin books, 1992), 119-193, quoted in Grenz, *A Primer on Postmodernism*, 51.

191 James B. Miller, "The Emerging Postmodern World," in *Postmodern Theology: Christian Faith in a Pluralist World*, ed. Frederic Burnham (San Francisco: Harper & Row, 1989), 10, quoted in Grenz, *A Primer on Postmodernism*, 53.

192 Dave Tomlinson, *The Post-Evangelical* (Grand Rapids, MI: Zondervan, 2003), 75 quoted in Sam Sam George, *Understanding the Coconut Generation* (Niles, IL: Mall Publishing, 2006), 202.

193 Adapted from Robert E. Webber, *The Younger Evangelicals* (Grand Rapids MI: Baker Books, 2002), 54.

194 Grenz, *A Primer on Postmodernism, 163-167*.

195 Eric Stanford, "The New Wave of Gen X Churches: Get Your Glimpse of the Future Here," *Next Wave*, http://www.next-wave.org/dec99/new_wave_of_gen_x_churches.htm (accessed May 6, 2010).

196 Webber, *The Younger Evangelicals, 117-123*.

197 Robert E. Webber, *Ancient Future Evangelism* (Grand Rapids, MI: Baker Books, 2003), 60.

198 Webber, *Ancient Future Evangelism, 62*.

199 Grenz, *A Primer on Postmodernism, 168*.

200 Grenz, *A Primer on Postmodernism, 172*.

201 Webber, *Ancient Future Evangelism*, 55-69.

202 George, *Understanding the Coconut Generation*, 203.

Part Three

Strategies and Methods for Introducing Jesus

Eight

General Principles that Make a Missional Church

A church does not become evangelistic by accident. At the same time, evangelism is not just for a select few churches. Instead, it is the calling of every church. It is easier for the church to be inward looking and focus on members that are familiar than to invest time, money, and effort in dealing with those outside. It is not difficult for a church that has never been involved in evangelism to turn around and become an evangelistic church. The following are some principles that will enable any church to make that certain turn.

LEADERSHIP PRINCIPLES

MISSIONAL OBJECTIVE

This is the point at which every church ought to begin, the point at which the church asks itself, "What is the mission to which God is calling us?" Once the mission is defined, it should be articulated well so that everybody knows it and not just the leadership of the church. To define the mission is to answer the why question.

To answer the "why?" question, we have to know the reason why the person or organization exists. Answering why is the first step in writing a purpose statement. Knowing why is a key responsibility of effective leadership. An old maxim claims that "He who knows how will always have a job; he who knows why will always be his boss"….Vision should begin with an answer to the why question.[203]

Vision is beyond just knowing the purpose. It is answering the "What if" question. What if the church accomplished its purpose, where would it be ten years from now? Vision requires imagining the future, based on the purpose of the church. The challenge of visionary leadership is to "gather all the vision from inside and outside the organization, extract the best that matches the purpose, and then craft a vision statement that will unify the people in moving toward the common goal and a more desirable future."[204] The church leadership needs to talk constantly about the purpose and vision so that all the church members know exactly where in the church is in the plan of God.

STRONG, EMPOWERING LEADERSHIP

The pastor should facilitate and model magnetic congregational qualities. One of the more important functions of the pastor is as a vision-caster. A leader should have the vision and should be able to articulate it well. Other important traits of the leader are to keep evangelism as the main thing by making time and energy for it; be enthusiastic with a sense of humor and a positive attitude; exercise the skill of listening well; and spend time with God.[205]

While pastors of growing churches are not usually extroverts, they are more relationship and people oriented than those in declining churches. These pastors enable their members to fulfill the potential that God has for them instead of using them as pawns in fulfilling the grandiose vision that the pastor has. Thus, their goal orientation is based on their people orientation. When the pastor is not seen as the ultimate leader within whom lies the vision and the total theological interpretation, he is more likely to have a mentor of his own, usually some from outside the church.[206] This type of leadership runs contrary to the traditional top-down leadership and instead sees church members as co-workers. Then, everybody including the pastor is accountable to others.

The pastor should not confuse administration with leadership. Administration happens after leadership. A vision needs to be cast before it is implemented.[207] In addition, the pastor needs to manage the four usual responses in the church to evangelism: 25 percent are negative towards evangelism – they are against it; 25 percent are apathetic – they think its not for them; 49.5 percent want evangelism but do not know how to do it; and 0.5 percent of them have the gift of evangelism.[208]

The best kind of leadership is one in which decision-making is participatory. It is impossible and time consuming to get complete consensus on every issue. However, the more people that are involved in decision making, the more people that will own the decision.

RELATIONAL PRINCIPLES

ESTABLISH A CULTURE OF LOVING RELATIONSHIPS

The culture of the church is established initially by the pastor and subsequently by its members. Both the pastor and the members need to exhibit genuine love to visitors. Schwartz says,

There is a highly significant relationship between the ability of a church to demonstrate love and its long term growth potential. Growing churches possess on average a measurably higher "love quotient" than stagnant or declining ones. …It can be demonstrated that there is a significant connection between "laughter in the church" and that church's qualitative and numerical growth.…Unfeigned practical love has a divinely generated magnetic power far more effective than evangelistic programs which depend almost entirely on verbal communication. People do not want to hear us talk about love, they want to experience how Christian love really works.[209]

This is manifested not just on Sunday mornings, but also during the week – multiple interactions between church members unpressured by church leadership. This is important for people to want to come to the church week after week. This sense of community and oneness was characteristic of the early church.

The early church teaches us three principles for evangelism in a secular/ spiritual culture: we must be open to all; we are to preach, teach, enact and live an exclusive Christian message; and we need to create a community that not only looks after its own but cares for the needs of the world.[210]

EXHIBIT AN ATTITUDE OF "WELCOME HOME" FRIENDLINESS TOWARD NON-MEMBERS

Instead of the traditional church members vs. outsiders attitude that Christians are known to have, Charles Arn contends that, for effectiveness, the two in-gredients that should be in every service are the messages "you are loved" and "here is hope."[211] This attitude would naturally arise if one realizes that God many times begins his work in the unbeliever, even before he or she comes to church.

The leader needs to set the tone for the attitude of the church. The leader-ship team tends to emulate the emotional attitude of the leader and, in turn, the congregation reflects that attitude.[212] To enhance this, there need to be highly sanguine, overtly friendly members who will mingle with the crowd that comes in to the church – the "lobby lizards."[213] These people will convey the tone of the church to the newcomers. The availability of coffee and a nar-thex invites people to stay on and converse, even after the service has ended. This friendly atmosphere must be reflected in every ministry of the church, including the nursery and adult Sunday school classes.[214]

HOLISTIC SMALL GROUPS

The importance of small groups has been highlighted ever since the testimony of the expansive growth of Paul Yonggi Cho's church in Seoul, South Korea. Every church that is bigger than a large small group should have small groups. This is where Christians learn to live out the Christian faith – serving each other through the use of their gifts, bringing personal problems out for prayer and praise, exposition of Scripture and fellowship.

True church life should be worked out in small groups. The larger a church becomes, the more decisive the small groups are to sustain and in-fluence further growth.[215] The more a church consciously attempts to grow and multiply small groups, the more members will be close knit and like a family.

ADMINISTRATIVE PRINCIPLES

PROGRAMS

It is a known fact that no church can do everything well. However, all churches can do some things well. No one church can minister to all groups of people the exact same way. Thus, the church needs to find one or two programs that they can do excellently. These one or two programs should be extremely competent, so much so that the church is known for those programs. It is important that the competence of those programs be measured by the standards of competence in the community, and not by comparing it to other churches or to other programs within the same church. Obviously, those programs should meet the felt need of the community. When the local community recognizes the excellence of the programs that the church offers, other programs in the church also are perceived as being good. In addition, other programs in the church grow in excellence because of the standard set by the major programs. Any time a church plans to have an excellent program, it needs to give about four to five years of hard work to build it up.[216]

When a program meets the needs of the community and is part of the broad vision of the church, then the people who are attracted to it will eventually get to be a part of the church. If a church has a great youth center that is better than what the community offers, then youth are more likely to come to the church and, by proximity and familiarity, have a better chance of attending church than otherwise.

NEED-ORIENTED EVANGELISM

The church needs to begin evangelism based on the felt needs of the unchurched. Knowing the needs of the different subgroups of attendees and finding ways by which the church can satisfy them will result in an evangelistic outpouring. This was the evangelistic approach of the Son of God:

Whenever Jesus encountered a person he'd begin with their hurts, needs, and interests. When he sent His disciples out he told them to do the same..... When you are in pain either physically or emotionally, you aren't interested in the meanings of Greek and Hebrew words. You just want to get well.[217]

The four basic needs of a curious church attendee are a yearning to feel understood in the church, a yearning to understand in the church, a yearning to belong in the church, and a yearning for hope in the church.[218] Small congregations are primarily people centered, medium-sized congregations are activity centered, and large churches are event centered. Yet all churches should be able to give opportunities for people to participate in the church. The best way to facilitate this is by helping people to be involved in a group and have a job to do in church. Without this, 90 percent of new people will become inactive in one year. There are usually sixty jobs available in church for every one hundred people. The church should list out all the ministries and all the people that are needed for each job so that those who are interested can sign up. Similarly, new members should be part of a specific group, like the adult Sunday school. Of the members who are natural leaders, about 15 percent will want to be in a leadership role at some point, or they will leave the church. Thus, ministry as well as management jobs should be created.[219]

There are six groups of singles – young working adults; young college adults; young, never married, post college aged adults; young, previously married adults twenty-five to thirty-five years of age; previously married adults thirty-five to fifty-five years of age; and those over fifty-five, who are divorced, widowed, or never married. There needs to be specific ministry directed at each of these groups for them to get involved. None of these groups can be mixed together. For example, the four greatest needs of old age are: health, financial security, a closer relationship with God, and a closer relationship with family to counter the common complaint of loneliness. Any attempts at maintaining contact with seniors will meet a large need.[220]

INVITE PEOPLE

Since people progress from becoming worship service visitors to attendees to members, every church should learn to attract large numbers of first-time visitors. Seventy to ninety percent of people who join a church come because of a personal invitation. Only 12.3 percent of new members are influenced to join by a church's location. People choose their churches the same way they choose their friends – because of the relationship they have with someone who invites them to attend. That is why the new members are the best inviters.[221] People tend to invite when their own faith is growing, when they like the pastor, and when they are excited about what is happening in their congregation.[222]

Ninety-five percent of all effective evangelistic interactions involve planting, not harvesting. The harvesting never happens on the same day and is rarely done by the same person. Thus, most of the evangelistic activity occurs outside the church among natural relationships between people. Each Christian has on average 8.5 contacts with non-Christians. Thus, there is no necessity to encourage more contact with other non-Christians. Instead, the focus should be to use already existing relationships for evangelism.[223] The church should intentionally tap into this relationship network and create a system by which people can invite their friends. The use of systematic invitation plans increases even the number of spontaneous invitations. Even though personal invitation is ideal, less ideal invitations can be offered also, by personal delivery letters, open house invitations, a visible church building and sign, an ad in the yellow pages, radio, television, direct mail, and newspaper, and specifically targeting new residents.[224]

DEVELOP EFFECTIVE WAYS TO ENCOURAGE FIRST-TIME VISITORS TO RETURN

Herb Miller advocates a house visit of first time visitors as being much more effective than mail or a phone call.

When lay persons make fifteen-minute visits to the homes of first-time worship visitors within thirty-six hours, 85 percent of them return the following week. Make this home visit within seventy-two hours and 60 percent of them return. Make it seven days later and 15 percent will return. The pastor making this call, rather than laypersons, cuts each result in half.[225]

Callahan opines that there would be adequate visitation in a two-hundred-member church if there were twenty visits a week with church members, twenty visits with non-church members, and adequate hospital visitation.[226] This entails that the church obtain the names and addresses of all visitors. Care must be taken that visitors are not singled out to do any task – including standing up, filling forms, announcing themselves – since most people prefer to remain anonymous when in a new place.

SOUND CHURCH STRUCTURE

This section is not about the physical structure, but the administrative structure of the church. There is a view that assumes that structure and life are mutually exclusive, and, in a church setting, it is better to opt for spiritual life instead of spiritual structure. However, that is contrary to life as it is observed in the created world. Every living being has a specific structure; indeed, it is that structure that brings life.[227]

There needs to be an organizational structure for church leadership and church ministry, with heads for each sub ministry that is focused and driven. The Apostle Paul wrote about several strata of leadership in the church because he knew the importance of systematic organization. Of course, it is possible to be so engrossed in the maintaining of the structure that life and growth is stunted.

SPIRITUAL PRINCIPLES

WORSHIP SERVICE

The church should have a worship service that stirs warmth in the congregation, gives a strong sense of otherness, has a strong music program, and has preaching from conviction. Music is critical to the service.

The style of music you choose to use in your services will be one of the most critical decisions you make in the life of your church. It may also be the most influential factor in determining who your church reaches for Christ and whether or not your church grows. You must match your music to the kind of people God wants your church to reach.[228]

The church should first find out who their target congregation is and then find out the kind of music that that target group listens to. The sermon is not just the message anymore; the entire service is. It is essential to know the target audience of the worship service and then consider how the worship service can move those people into the very presence of God and instill the awe of the holy other. According to Charles Arn, "The sermon speaks to the mind; drama speaks to the heart; music speaks to the soul. Ultimately it is the effective interaction of all three that best communicates the message God wants us to share."[229]

The church should develop variety in the worship service. Scheduling two morning services is one of the best ways to add variety. Adding a second service usually increases total attendance by 5 to 15 percent. The more options the church has, the more responses it can get from people. People assimilate knowledge in three different ways – visual, auditory, and kinesthetic. Thus, it behooves the pastor to have a worship service that uses all three kinds of communication – seeing, hearing, and touching. Fifty-five percent of a speaker's impact comes from visual qualities, thirty-eight percent from auditory qualities, and seven percent from the content of the talk.[230]

People come once to church because of a friend's judgment. They return for a second look because of their own judgment. Around 10 percent of people join a church because a friend is a part of that church. The quality of the worship service is the reason why people join a church 83 percent of the time. If the worship service does not meet the needs of the first-time visitor, no amount of friendliness can convince them to join.[231] Of course, one church's worship service cannot be duplicated at another's. Each church needs a worship service that is indigenous to the target group that it is trying to reach. There are many kinds of worship services in the myriad of churches. Many churches follow several models that have worked in other churches. However, the key factor that makes a worship service attractive in any place at any time is the presence of the Holy Spirit, enabling and inspiring the worshippers.[232] This goes beyond the motions of spiritual activity that is done on a Sunday morning. Instead, it is the giving up of the worship service to the empowering and filling of the Holy Spirit. When people are able to connect to the holy other in each worship service, they are inspired far beyond what any sermon or song can achieve.

PASSIONATE SPIRITUALITY

The church should emphasize and live out genuine spirituality. A pastor and a leadership team that is really spiritual will stimulate spirituality in the congregation. The church should concentrate on nurturing the spiritual side of human personality. Even though evangelism has got to be need based, the final purpose is to nurture the spiritual life of the attendee. Growing churches recognize this need as the most important.

Growing churches give people more than psychological help, more than good ideas, more than emotional experiences, more than a social group. They take seriously the spiritual side of human personality. They do not confuse the bread of life with the crumbs of religion.[233]

Evangelism and church growth should be beyond mere programs and activities, beyond mere civic religion, beyond rationalism, beyond emotionalism, beyond ecumenical universalism, beyond institutionalism, beyond Christian unity, beyond social action, beyond mere principles, beyond conservatism. Rather, since God's kingdom is a spiritual realm, the spiritual aspect of a person's life should be the main focus. This is done by emphasizing personal devotion, prayer, Bible reading, and practicing the presence of God.[234] Church development is not dependent on either spiritual styles or certain spiritual practices. The point of separation between growing and non-growing churches is whether they are on fire, enthusiastic, and passionate about their spirituality. In contrast are those churches in which legalism is the driving force behind their actions. Some areas of spiritual discipline that are indicators of spiritual passion are prayer and Bible reading and how the church member views the experience. If it is an inspiring experience to spend time in prayer and communion with God, then it is reflective of the spiritual passion that one has had. This enthusiasm, then, overflows into the area of evangelism, and people are more likely to invite friends to church.[235]

BIBLICAL PREACHING AND TEACHING

It is easy for a pastor to digress into giving popular opinions, political views, or purely social justice issues. People now expect to hear a biblical sermon. They are tired of the liberal interpretation of spirituality and desire biblically based, theologically conservative opinions based on Scripture. The pastor needs to preach relevant messages that fulfill the needs of listeners. Also, the pastor can preach about unbibilical doctrines, based on sensationalism and emotionalism. However, what is essential is an accurate interpretation and delivery of God's word.

Speakers also need to be aware that church members are not seminary students and usually do not have a historical view of different doctrines. Thus, a pastor who speaks in theological jargon and complex critical arguments, proving and counter-proving irrelevant issues, has missed connecting with his hearers. Lay members desire to hear the plain, simple word of God.

GIFT ORIENTED MINISTRY

Every person on the pastoral staff should be doing the work that he or she is gifted for and should do it because he or she is called to do it in that church. There should be no other reason. The church should always be on the lookout for people with gifts and encourage them to use their time in the church. Every person is expected to know and work on the strengths that they have for the benefit of the church.

The gift-oriented approach reflects the conviction that God sovereignly determines which Christians should best assume which ministries. The role of church leadership is to help its members to identify their gifts and to integrate them into appropriate ministries. When Christians serve in their area of giftedness, they generally function less in their own strength and more in the power of the Holy Spirit. Probably no factor influences the contentedness of Christians more than whether they are utilizing their gifts. When members' personal ministry involvement matches their gifts and when those in ministry get adequate training from the church to perform those functions, the church increases in quality and grows.[236]

The research that Schwartz and his team did disproves a thesis commonly held in evangelistically active groups: that "every Christian is an evangelist."... It is indeed the responsibility of every Christian to use his or her own specific gifts in fulfilling the great commission. This does not, however, make him or her an evangelist. Evangelists are only those to whom God has given the corresponding spiritual gift… [confirming] C. Peter Wagner's thesis that the gift of evangelism applies to no more than ten percent of all Christians.[237]

Instead of attempting to use gifts that one does not possess, especially the gift of evangelism, the responsibility of each Christian is to use the gifts he or she has to serve non-Christians and use the basis of that relationship to invite them to church where other church members with other gifts, including that of evangelism, can cause the process of evangelism to continue.

FUNCTIONAL PRINCIPLES

VISIBILITY AND ACCESSIBILITY

Every church needs to be visible so that people can recognize it. A church that is hidden attracts fewer people than a church that is highly visible. If the church is visible to people when they are not looking for a church, people will remember about it when they are looking for one. No one will remember a church that they have not seen before. In addition to optical visibility, the church also needs community visibility. If the church is publicly visible, then the pastors and leaders of the church will be recognized in the life of the community. The greatest method for gaining visibility is to have people who have been served by the church make the church visible to their relational circle.[238]

Another important concept is that of accessibility. The church needs to be accessible to people. Those who wish to visit the church should be able to easily get in and out of the church. Even though the pastoral staff spends a lot of time within the walls of the church, they should be aware of the physical condition of the church location and facilities. Importantly, accessibility is also about the pastor and the staff being accessible to people. People are more likely to feel welcome and thus be a part of the church if they feel that the pastor and the members are open and available.[239]

PARKING, LANDSCAPING, AND FACILITIES

It is important for newcomers to see that there is space available for them. A packed parking lot is as unwelcoming as an uncomfortably crowded church.

Charles Arn says:

The rule of thumb is one parking stall for every 2.5 people you expect in the service. The well-known 80 percent rule also applies to parking lots; that is if your parking lot is filled to 80% or more for four months, it is unlikely that additional growth will occur.[240]

Also, the most effective parking is within one block of the church. There needs to be a parking supervisor who is friendly and welcoming by nature. His role is very important since he is the first person that a visitor sees.[241]

As far as facilities go, Schaller contends that the two critical areas that give a good first impression are the nursery and the women's restroom.[242] It is important for the church leadership to pay attention to the maintenance of church facilities since the state of the structure gives an impression to a newcomer. A well-kept building gives a different impression than a run down structure.[243]

FINANCIAL RESOURCES

Although not the most important factor in evangelism, finance is a necessary matter. After all, any evangelistic initiative requires finances to start and to maintain.

A responsible theology of stewardship encourages local congregations to invest money in such a way as to (1) increase missional services in the community, (2) maximize the effectiveness of the local church and (3) add to the number of households that contribute financially to the life and mission of the congregation. It is not the task of the church to save money. Nor is it the task of the church to spend money. Rather, it is vitally important that the church invest its funds wise.[244]

It is important for the pastor and the church leadership to plan their finances for the future of the church and find ways to generate more funds. Even though it is God who will supply all the needs of the church, He usually supplies it through people. The church, then, needs to be intelligent about the money it collects, the money it uses, and the ways that the money is collected.

When raising finances, it must be remembered that people give money to a defined mission. Thus, the mission of the church needs to be articulated before the money can be raised. Also, people give to people first, and to programs and plans later. Thus, the most effective means of raising funds for evangelism is relational.[245]

Even though there are many principles that make a church evangelistic, most of these principles fall into place as soon as the church becomes passionate about evangelism. When the entire focus of the church is directed towards evangelism, then all other programs within the church become more effective.

Notes:

203 Leith Anderson, *Leadership That Works* (Minneapolis, MN: Bethany House Pub.,1999), 193.

204 Anderson, *Leadership That Works,* 197.

205 Herb Miller, *How to Build a Magnetic Church* (Nashville, TN: Abingdon Press, 1987), 114-119.

206 Christian A. Schwarz, *Natural Church Development: A Guide to Eight Essential Qualities of Healthy Churches* (Saint Charles, IL: Churchsmart Resources, 1996), 22-23.

207 Miller, *How to Build a Magnetic Church,* 117.

208 Miller, *How to Build a Magnetic Church,* 115.

209 Schwarz, *Natural Church Development,* 36.

210 Weber, *Ancient Future Evangelism,* 57.

211 Charles Arn, *How to Start a New Service* (Grand Rapids, MI: Baker Books, 1997), 155-156.

212 Daniel Goleman, *Primal Leadership* (Boston, MA: Harvard Business School Press, 2004).

213 Leith Anderson, "Leading and Managing Your Ministry" (lecture, Fuller Theological Seminary, January 31- February 4, 2005).

214 Miller, *How to Build a Magnetic Church,* 68-70.

215 Schwarz, *Natural Church Development,* 32-33.

216 Kennon L. Callahan and Ian B. Tanner, *Twelve Keys to an Effective Church* (San Francisco, CA: Jossey-Bass, 1997), 64-70.

217 Rick Warren, *The Purpose Driven Church* (Grand Rapids, MI: Zondervan Publishing, 1995), 197.

218 Robert L Randall, *What People Expect from Church* (Nashville, TN: Abingdon Press, 1992).

219 Miller, *How to Build a Magnetic Church,* 86-92.

220 Miller, *How to Build a Magnetic Church,* 93-98.

221 Miller, *How to Build a Magnetic Church,* 32-33.

222 Lyle Schaller in Miller, *How to Build a Magnetic Church,* 34.

223 Schwarz, *Natural Church Development,* 35.

224 Miller, *How to Build a Magnetic Church,* 33-43.

225 Miller, *How to Build a Magnetic Church,* 72-73.

226 Callahan, *Twelve Keys to an Effective Church,* 11.

227 Schwartz, *Natural Church Development,* 28-29.

228 Warren, *The Purpose Driven Church,* 280.

229 Arn, *How to Start a New Service*, 167.

230 Miller, *How to Build a Magnetic Church*, 52-56.

231 Miller, *How to Build a Magnetic Church*, 45.

232 Schwarz, *Natural Church Development*, 30-31.

233 Miller, *How to Build a Magnetic Church*, 101.

234 Miller, *How to Build a Magnetic Church*, 101-111.

235 Schwarz, *Natural Church Development*, 26-27.

236 Schwarz, *Natural Church Development*, 24-25.

237 Schwarz, *Natural Church Development*, 34.

238 Callahan, *Twelve Keys to an Effective Church*, 78-85.

239 Callahan, *Twelve Keys to an Effective Church*, 72-76.

240 Callahan, *Twelve Keys to an Effective Church*, 147.

241 Callahan, *Twelve Keys to an Effective Church*, 87-91.

242 Lyle Schaller, *44 Ways to Increase Your Church Attendance* (Nashville, TN: Abingdon Press, 1988), 92.

243 Callahan, *Twelve Keys to an Effective Church*, 97.

244 Callahan, *Twelve Keys to an Effective Church*, 106.

245 Callahan, *Twelve Keys to an Effective Church*, 111-112.

Nine

Strategies for Introducing Jesus

The target of evangelistic attempts conclusively determines the type of strategy that needs to be used. Pastor Rick Warren of the Saddleback church says,

The kind of fish you want to catch will determine every part of your strategy... There is no "one-size-fits-all" approach to fishing. Each demands a unique strategy. .. The same is true in fishing for men – it helps to know what you're fishing for.[246]

There cannot be one common method that is meant to reach every subgroup that exists among Enterans and Indericans. There need to be different points of entry for all of them to come in. However the basic characteristics of an Indian family are unique. A stereotypical Indian family in America would look like the Patel family.

THE INDIAN IMMIGRANT FAMILY

Vikram Patel was born near Mumbai, India in 1955. He completed his medical training at Mumbai Medical College and came to New York a year later, where he completed a residency in nephrology. Most of his extended family, including his two sisters, still live in India. After he settled down into his practice in New York, he returned to India and married a woman named Padma in a marriage arranged by his family. Padma came back to New York with

Vikram. Even though she was a graduate in commerce, she decided to stay at home and take care of the family, which over time grew to five with the addition of two daughters and a son. Vikram fully intended to return to India after he had become financially secure and was able to support his parents back home.

Every time Vikram's parents came to New York for a visit, they urged him to return to India. However, the months turned into years, and twenty-seven years later, Vikram Patel was still in America and had become acclimatized. In his heart of hearts, he knew that he would have a very difficult time re-adjusting to life in India. He had tried to persuade his parents to live in America, but they find it difficult to adjust to a new life and prefer to retire in their native land. Years ago, they were able to visit every few years, but in recent times their health has not permitted them to undertake the long journey to America. In addition, as the children grew up and started college, Vikram and his family were unable to go to India as often as before. Thus, Vikram and his family began to see less and less of their family in India.

The Patel family connected with Indian friends on weekends. They made it a point to visit the Swami Narayana Temple in Flushing, New York, every Saturday. Vikram found a group of friends with whom he managed to play cricket once in a while. Even though he enjoyed his work at his medical group, he occasionally felt isolated. Deep down he believed that it was because of his race; however, he chose to stand back and see the big picture – he was very well off in a foreign land. He wondered if his children would feel like misfits as they grew up.

Padma made sure to teach her children Hindu mythology. In India, she had not been very interested in going to the temple, but, once she arrived in the States, the temple was a good way to be connected with the Indian community, and it helped satisfy her spiritual needs. With the exception of work-related parties, it is very rare for Vikram and Padma to go out for a social event with non-Indians. Their desire to connect with Indians grew more and more as their visits to India became less and less.

The older children, Sonali and Amy, made their way into medical school and the youngest, Kevin, is still in college. He desires to be a high school teacher. Sonali, the oldest, married a doctor from Detroit, Michigan, who was a distant contact known to their family in India. Even though she was not completely convinced of the idea, she wanted to please her parents and so went along with the idea of marrying an Indian. Her parents' initial opinion was for their children to marry directly from India. The longer they stayed in America, though, the more open they became to the idea of marrying from America. However, they insisted that Sonali marry a Hindu Indian, and Sonali obliged.

Amy is twenty-two and insists that she is not going to marry an Indian. There have been many heated family conversations regarding this issue. In India, Vikram and Padma would have looked at caste, sub-caste, and astrology when it came to marriage, but in America, they are fine with anyone as long as he is an Indian Hindu. Amy, though, insists that she wants to marry an American, and her parents suspect that she might already have a boyfriend. Even though they may eventually reluctantly agree, at the same time, they are also concerned as to what kind of "baggage" an American spouse might carry. They have heard the different relationship issues that their American contacts have been through and wonder if the negative effects of those relationships would spill over into a marriage. Even though Sonali was interested in going to the temple with her parents, neither Amy nor Kevin was too keen on it once they grew up. They preferred to spend their Saturdays with friends or visiting the city.

Vikram and Padma are concerned about Kevin. They had wanted him to attend professional school, but he has been adamant in his dislike for prolonged education. The numerous conversations and cajoling did not work. Kevin attempted engineering school for a year and dropped out, disinterested. That was when Vikram and Padma realized that it is better for him to pursue any education rather than no education.

Even though the children listened to Bollywood songs and watched Indian movies with their parents when growing up, their interests have changed significantly. Not only do they not watch Indian programs any longer, but they express their dislike for them. They currently prefer to listen to alternative and pop-rock genres and watch American entertainment exclusively. They hardly meet any Indians and are uninterested in their parents' religion. Communication between the children and parents is minimal – needs are expressed and needs are fulfilled. Eventually, the only conversations between parents and children concerned losing weight, respecting elders, pursuing education, or the "dangers" of being too American. As they became more and more American and less and less Indian, the children had little in common with their parents. There was almost nothing that either group agreed on.

The Patel children grew up without any significant lack of money and have had a very comfortable life. It is to the amazement of their American friends that they drive in nice cars that their parents bought for them and have unlimited access to their parents' money. It is very likely that they will not have any outstanding student loans that they need to pay for later. Their parents have told them that any amount of money will be spent for education, and it is understood that they stay with the parents until and even after marriage, as long as they please.

As the children attended school, they were aware of their different color. They came to realize that there was not just a physical difference from their friends, but indeed many things that they were familiar with at home were different from what their American friends were accustomed to. There were many cultural differences. Growing up, they grew weary of explaining why they could not participate in sleepovers, stay out late with friends, or be set up on dates. Often, they wished that they had never been born into an Indian family. However, as they grew mature, they warmed to their rich cultural history, causing the antagonism to diminish. They even talked to their American friends with Indian pride whenever an Indian was recognized in the media. However, they have no desire to go back to India for a visit and would at the most tolerate some Indian foods or events. They have done their best to make American-ness and Indian-ness co-exist.

This is the target group—a typical Indian family that the church in America needs to evangelize. Even though there are many exceptions to the general stereotypical Indian family, the basic structure and core characteristics are largely the same. However, it is the many variations within each Enteran and Inderican group that exhibit differences in receptivity to the gospel.

RECEPTIVITY

People are receptive to the gospel more at certain times than at others. Instead of spending limited resources on those who are not ready to listen, the church needs to focus on those who are interested. "If a home or town refuses to welcome you or listen to you, leave that place and shake its dust off your feet" (Matt. 10:14). Indericans are more receptive to the gospel than Enterans because they are less connected to their parents' religion, they are in a pre-evangelistic state thanks to the Christian American culture, they are open to new ideas, and their postmodern thinking precludes them from segregation.

The different groups are broadly Enteran and Inderican. Subsets of these groups are placed in increasing order of their receptivity. Tables 9.1 and 9.2 list these specific subsets for Enterans and Indericans respectively.

Table 9.1. Enteran groups

Group	Description
Earlier immigrants	This group has seen the America of the last quarter of the previous century and have seen the hippie movement, the grunge effect and have reason to shun Christianity. They have learned to co-exist as a Hindu in a predominantly Christian culture. They may be the least receptive.
Non-working relatives of immigrants	Those who have come to America on a family visa. Since they are not working, exposure to American and Christian culture is limited.
Traditional and nationalistic Hindus	
Those involved in evangelistic Hinduism	Example: International Society for Krishna Consciousness (ISKCON)
Secular Hindus	
Those residing in states with fewer Indians	
Recent immigrants	Those who have moved from India and those who have recently moved within America
Those seeking jobs	Including relatives or spouses of earlier immigrants
Those in professional schools	Including those that haven't immigrated to America, but have come on a student visa
Those following *Bhakti Marga*	
Those at crossroads in life	Divorcees, widowed, newly single etc

Table 9.2. Inderican groups

Group	Description
Marginalists	Low Indian-ness, Low American-ness (LILA)
Traditionalists	High Indian-ness, Low American-ness (HILA)
Those of marriageable age	Depending on the person, the Inderican of marriageable age can be either more inclined to look towards Hinduism or be more open toward non-Hindu alliances.
Secular	
Job seekers	
Students	
Biculturals	High Indian-ness, High American-ness (HIHA)
Assimilationists	Low Indian-ness, High American-ness (LIHA).
Special needs	Including drug and alcohol addictions
Dissatisfied with parental and familial expectations	

NEEDS AND INTERESTS

Once the various groups have been identified, the diverse needs of these groups should be discovered and fulfilled. Meeting needs is the primary way that Jesus interacted with his listeners. He did not merely preach the heavenly word and walk away. He connected to people first at their point of physical need and then gave them the spiritual food that they yearned for. These are the general needs of the two main groups of Indians in America.

THE NEEDS OF ENTERANS

The new immigrants' primary need is community. Enterans need culture, community, and the segregation of language. It is important for Enterans to meet other Enterans who speak the same Indian language. Thus, churches need to be started in different Indian languages, maintaining the linguistic and sub-cultural segregations.

Enterans also need to engage in Indian cultural activities. They will get this need fulfilled only if they live in states that have a large community of Indians who celebrate Indian events and festivals. Unfortunately, many Indian churches, both in India and America, shun the celebration of Indian festivals because they have confused them with Hindu festivals and have thus refused to fulfill this cultural need of the Enteran.

Addressing the need of acculturation, there are many Enteran students who are in America on a student visa with very little family nearby. Their need is to be able to get around and to learn and adapt to the culture. In the past, there was a need for organizations to show aspects of American culture to new immigrant Indians. However, since there are many more Indians in America now than before, the current Indian population is capable of introducing other Indians to the new culture. However, the need remains among students. The ministry of International Student Inc. fulfills this need.

Many Enterans who are at the crossroads of life due to various circumstances need to find a place of welcome. The Indian culture unfortunately and inadvertently shuns Enterans who have been widowed or divorced. Their greatest need, then, is to be welcomed into a community. Unfortunately, the Indian church puts legalistic adherence to biblical doctrine on a higher pedestal than evangelism and completely shuts the door on this need.

Enterans' need for security is acute. Hindus know from experience that the predictions of the astrologer may or may not come true. Still, they continue to seek after sources who can give some insight into the future. The certainty of the Christian faith offers that sure hope.[247]

Shame creates needs, too. The effects of sin on Adam and Eve were guilt and shame. Interestingly, the western society is a guilt-based society, the Eastern society is shame based, and the Middle East is fear/honor based. Thus the Enteran comes from a shame-based background while the Inderican grows in a guilt-based setting.

Guilt is the self condemnation resulting from the violation of internalized convictions of right and wrong; whereas shame is the feeling of group condemnation resulting from an unexpected societal or divine norm. Guilt is a feeling and/or condition occurring when one has broken or not kept a divine or human law. On the other hand, shame is a feeling and/or condition resulting form a shortcoming in one's state of being either before peers, somebody high in the social hierarchy, or even God.[248]

The need, then, for the Enteran struggling with shame is adoption, the need for the American struggling with guilt is justification, while, for the Inderican struggling with guilt and shame, it is both.

THE NEEDS OF INDERICANS

In spite of their similarities with Enterans, the needs of Indericans are vastly different. Many Indian churches, not recognizing this difference, tend to think that Indericans will eventually "grow out" of their "immaturity."

Indericans need meaningful community, more than Enterans do. They also need meaningful relationships that are authentic. Even though both Enterans and Indericans need community, the type of community each needs, is different. Enterans need Indian community while Indericans need eclectic community.

Counseling is needed, too. Indericans are Gen Xers who matured too late, and now suddenly life has thrust itself on them, requiring them to rise to the challenge. They need advice on how to live life. They fear rejection and loneliness, are concerned about providing for themselves and their families, and wonder if they can balance work and family well. Their biggest need is to be guided through "competent parenting" and family life. They also need answers to their questions of identity.

Indericans are on a discovery course to find where they really belong. This problem is acute in the Inderican who is neither a complete American nor a complete Indian. The longing to belong and the sense of security it can provide are fundamental to all but more pronounced in hybrid generations.[249]

There is pervasive loneliness among Indericans. They are excluded from their parents' generation as well as from mainstream Americans – double marginalization – on account of ethnicity and generational differences.[250] The same fate that befell the Gen X group affects the Inderican. Parents of the Gen Xers – the Baby Boomers – were so involved in establishing a life for themselves and for their children that they inadvertently ignored their children. Similarly, Enterans, by virtue of being strangers in a foreign land and with the necessity to make a living, adapted a similar lifestyle. They overworked, saved, and sacrificed for the sake of their children and were not able to spend time with them. This resulted in Indericans being disconnected from their parents. Consequently, they experience loneliness. Churches should incorporate intentional times of fellowship during church and small group gatherings.

In addition to the workaholic mentality of the Enterans, there is tremendous pressure placed on Indericans to perform with academic excellence. Every Enteran parent is likely to decide what their children are supposed to do when they grow up. Their future usually involves higher education. Thus, Indericans live with the attitude of inadequacy, being compared with other Indericans.

In terms of marriage, young Indian women will continue to face difficulty in finding Indian mates for a variety of reasons. First, there are 114 women for every 100 men between fifteen and twenty-four years of age. Second, generally men who have grown up in America are open to marrying girls from India, but the converse is not true. Many Inderican girls are not willing to be a traditional wife to an Enteran from India.[251]

Additionally, Indericans struggle with many addictions: alcohol, materialism, drugs, gambling, sex, and pornography.[252] The stigma of having an addiction is indelible in the Indian setting. For example, it is easy for an American pastor to announce that he has had a pornographic problem in the past, but, if an Indian pastor ever said that, he could never be the pastor of an Indian church again. There is a strong stigma associated with sexual, drug, and alcohol issues. Hence, Indericans keep such issues in secret so that neither their parents nor their churches would know. Also, even if the parents are cognizant of a sexual or substance abuse problem, they will never seek help from the church or an Indian organization for fear of rejection. Churches that do not have addiction counseling programs should collaborate with parachurch organizations that deal with these issues.

Sex is a taboo topic, as well, in the Indian household, and very few people speak openly about it. Everyone is expected to hold on to traditional values. However, being in America has changed that view toward sex. Sam George says that youth leaders across the country confirm that sexual sin and abuse are common in the Indian community. Young people think that sexual behavior is a matter of personal choice and tend to get their ideology from peers and media.[253] The concept of chastity and purity are considered to be traditional and Indian and therefore unappealing, while promiscuity is thought of as being progressive and American. The church should, therefore, organize discussions and candid talks on God's view of sex and sexuality.

MOVING FROM NEEDS TO THE GOSPEL

It is important to know about the needs of the people being evangelized. However, at some point, the issue of sin and the forgiveness that Jesus gives should be presented, even if it is not the immediate need of the individual. Evangelism is all about the forgiveness and salvation that Jesus brings.

In thinking about how a person can combine need-based conversation with the core issues of evangelism, Ben Johnson gives four biblical models of evangelism.[254] First is the *incarnational* model, emphasizing the immanence of Jesus Christ and His fellowship with humans. Second is the *atonement* model, stressing the justice of God that resulted in the death of Christ and, thereby, forgiveness of humankind's sin. Third is the *eschatological* model, which puts forward the soon coming of Christ and end time events. Fourth is the *kingdom* model, which presents the eternal life that God gives to us now.

The key to facilitating the presentation of the gospel is to start with the felt need of the person, that is, the incarnational model, and slowly progress until the atonement model is reached. The evangelist should be aware of the needs of the person and should always start from there. This is the entry point. The introduction to Jesus at this point can be as teacher or friend or anything that fulfills the immediate need. However, as the person gets closer and closer to Christ, he or she experiences more and more of Jesus Christ and will eventually come into a personal relationship with Him. The goal of the evangelist is simply to introduce Christ to the person at any point that fulfills the immediate need.[255]

SPECIFIC EVANGELISTIC PRINCIPLES RELEVANT TO A HINDU[256]

CASTE

Caste hierarchy and divisions among Hindus continue to cause problems in the Church. Unfortunately, when the Roman Catholic and Protestant missionaries came to India, they did not completely eliminate the caste system from their churches. Instead, in order to influence more people, they continued the caste system within the church, with the higher and lower castes sitting on either side of the church. When they tried to reverse this later on, many of the upper castes left the church, and the church consisted predominantly of lower castes.

To this day, the perception is that Christianity is for the lower castes, resulting in a social stigma attached to becoming a Christian. Knowledge of this fact will explain much of the initial resistance Hindus have to the hearing of the gospel.

DEVOTION AND SPIRITUAL GIFTS

Since devotion to their gods is preeminent for Hindus, personal relationship and a devotion to Jesus Christ should be emphasized in the presentation of the gospel. It is easy for a Hindu to understand devotion and personal discipline. The personal nature of Jesus and his ability to fulfill one's personal needs should be emphasized.[257]

Hindus are also impressed by the healing powers of Jesus Christ. It is helpful to focus on the miracle narratives of Jesus in the Gospels and his ability to heal more than just diseases. They need to understand the importance and relevance of spiritual matters in day-to-day living.[258]

SUPERSTITION AND FAMILY STRUCTURE

Superstition in Hinduism is merely a socioeconomic and literacy issue. It is not a theological problem for Hindus since Hindu theology tolerates it. The main reason for this is the Hindu belief in karma and, therefore, fatalism. Thus, any opposition to superstition is seen as an affront to Hindu theology. In spite of this, it is possible for Christians to present the surety of the hope in Jesus Christ.[259] It is interesting that the pre-modern issue of superstition survived modernity and has existed to the cusp of postmodernism. Sadly, Hindu superstitious beliefs have penetrated the Church. There are many Christians who unknowingly follow Hindu superstitions, especially concerning auspicious times and dates. The surety of God's word can progressively quell the uncertainty of superstitions.

In addition to the lack of coercion when presenting Jesus to a Hindu, an evangelist needs to have patience to see any fruit. In general, conversion among Indians needs more time and patience. This is because, unlike the individualistic American, Indians are intricately intertwined with their families. Thus, conversion of the individual often involves conversations and, in some cases, conversion of the family itself.

GUIDANCE, FOCUS ON JESUS, AND ALLOW FOR THE SUPERNATURAL

Hindus, like everybody else, are interested in knowing the future, and Hindus do it by using astrology. When a person is born, an astrologer is consulted who maps out the person's life. Thus, for most major decisions in a Hindu's life – marriage or buying a new house – the astrologer informs the Hindu family if the stars are lined up appropriately for the best results. Even they know that many times the prediction may or may not be true. It is important for the Christian to talk about the constant personal presence of God in one's life and the continued guidance that He gives.

When stories of Jesus are told, it is important to avoid stories from the Old Testament or about Jesus in historical terms, limiting him geographically to Israel. It is important to focus on Jesus as God and the simple story of Jesus. Avoid talking about membership in a church or baptism or even about Hindu gods. Emphasis should be solely on devotion to Jesus as God.[260] It is important not to syncretize the person of Christ to fit into the Indian mindset to increase his acceptability. Also, it is important not to "hide" any of his claims.

Hindus need to see Christ just the way he is without any watering down or hyperbole of his personality.[261]

It is tempting for the evangelist to formulate arguments and counter arguments and attempt to point out inconsistencies in Hindu doctrine. This, coupled with the erroneous belief that Hinduism is a pagan religion, can cause a discussion to quickly degenerate into a nonsensical argument. It is better to wait and allow for the Holy Spirit to do his work in the heart of the Hindu. There is a place for philosophical and doctrinal discussion for a person with genuine questions. However, there are millions of Hindus who are being converted, not because of carefully constructed arguments, but on the basis of an encounter with Jesus.

CONCLUSION

Churches and individuals need to do whatever it takes to establish contact with the target group. The church cannot be immiscible to the culture and hope to impact it. The gospel and culture are symbiotic. "The gospel is always translated into a culture, and God's people are formed in that culture in response to the translated and spirit-empowered Word."[262] It requires that natural instincts be evaluated in the light of evangelism, with church members intentionally maintaining their friendships with Hindu Enterans and Indericans.

So if we're going to impact our world for Christ, the most effective approach will be through friendships with those who need to be reached. We'll have to get close to them so they can see that we genuinely care about them individually and that we have their best interests in mind. Over time, that will earn their trust and respect.[263]

For many churches, this is not first nature. However, with practice and effort, it is possible to adapt to a non-Christian culture within the boundaries of biblical truth.

In addition to reaching out to target groups, churches should be geared to welcome non-Christians who do not have a prior Christian background. Since there are different kinds of people, the welcome should include different options. People in America are used to having choices, and they expect the same from church too. Henry Ford offered the Model-T Ford in any color as long as that color was black, but that situation is long gone. It is sensible to use all kinds of approaches in all kinds of ways in all kinds of places to reach Enterans and Indericans. "I have become all things to all men so that by all possible means I might save some" (1 Corinthians 9:22).

There are many ways to introduce Jesus to both Enterans and Indericans. It is important to employ different methods and use a multi-faceted approach for each sub-group. The different methods are merely different conduits that enable different people groups to be able to listen to the one eternal gospel message.

Notes:

246 Warren, *The Purpose Driven Church*, 186-187.

247 Thirumalai, *Sharing Your Faith*, 99.

248 George, *Understanding the Coconut Generation*, 200.

249 George, *Understanding the Coconut Generation,* 92.

250 George, *Understanding the Coconut Generation*, 115.

251 George, *Understanding the Coconut Generation*, 121.

252 George, *Understanding the Coconut Generation*, 125.

253 George, *Understanding the Coconut Generation*, 116-117.

254 Ben Johnson, *An Evangelism Primer: Practical Principles for Congregations* (Louisville: Westminster John Knox Press 1983), 11-12, in Alphonse, "The Gospel and Hindu '*Bhakti*,'" 305-306.

255 The classic example is the way Jesus was progressively revealed to the Samaritan woman in John chapter 4.

256 Some points are from Ravi Zacharias, "The Spurious Glitter of Pantheism," Ravi Zacharias International Ministries, podcast, http://htod.cdncon.com/o2/rzimht/MP3/LMPT/147-3.mp3 (accessed May 8, 2010).

257 Thirumalai, *Sharing Your Faith with a Hindu*, 64-65.

258 Thirumalai, *Sharing Your Faith with a Hindu*, 65.

259 Thirumalai, *Sharing Your Faith with a Hindu*, 138-139.

260 Thirumalai, *Sharing Your Faith with a Hindu*, 65-66.

261 W. H. Thorp, "Indigenous Christianity," *Harvest Field* 14, no. 11 (1903): 405-418, in Alphonse, "The Gospel and Hindu '*Bhakti*,'" 165.

262 Darrell L. Guder, ed., *Missional Church* (Grand Rapids, MI: Eerdmans Publishing Co., 1998), 11.

263 Bill Hybels, *Becoming a Contagious Christian* (Grand Rapids, MI: Zondervan, 1994), 97.

Ten

Methods for Introducing Jesus

The two groups of Indians – Enterans and Indericans – need different sets of methods to be reached. There is not just one method to share the gospel, but multiple ones, and churches need to be intentional in reaching out to Hindus. Growth is an active process, not a passive one. "Churches that aggressively seek new members tend to grow. Passive congregations that assume moving members will seek them out tend to shrink."[264]

METHODS FOR INTRODUCING JESUS TO ENTERANS

WEEKEND RETREATS

The existence of Hindu ashrams (retreat centers) in India in the past had spawned the formation of Christian ashrams for the express purpose of evangelism. However, in recent history, there is a lack of interest among Indians, even for Hindu ashrams. However, the concept of retreating for the purpose of reflection and communion is an ancient idea that is worth exploring.

A modification of these ashrams was made by E. Stanley Jones in India. Instead of having people stay in the ashram for long periods of time, he had a few people come together to stay for one to two months, during which time they were presented with the gospel. He also had sessions for a few days or over the weekend, using a small group template for the purpose of spiritual revival. This method of evangelism can be modified in modern America as a weekend retreat for seekers or as a once a week program like the Alpha Course.

DIALOGUE[265]

In the not-so-distant past, the primary method of evangelism was a top-down homily in which the evangelist preached to the listeners. However, this kind of a method has been challenged. Now, the focus is more and more on a dialogue instead of a monologue. Even though dialogue with a Hindu can result in increased knowledge of Hindu faith for the Christian evangelist, it is important to keep in focus that evangelism is the primary goal.

E. Stanley Jones pioneered Round Table Conferences in India. He gathered together people from different religions and gave them all the same amount of time to talk about their religion. Three results came from this. First, the Christians' personal faith was enriched as they talked about their faith in the context of other faiths. Secondly, in articulating their personal experience of the meaningfulness and usefulness of their religious beliefs, it made a philosophical religion into an intensely practical one. It was essentially a time of testimony of one's personal experience with the faith. Thirdly, as the conversation went along, the moral and spiritual supremacy of Christ became obvious to everyone, and the rest of the conversation was compared with Christ as the yardstick. At the end of these talks, the supremacy of Christ towered over every one else.

Even though these dialogues can rarely be used for direct evangelism, it is predominantly a preparation for later evangelism. Thus, these conversations lead to relationships that can later result in evangelism. The goal behind these dialogues is to introduce Christ in a general way as being a part of the Christian's daily life.

The opportunity to talk to people in the context of their worship, and to enable them to cultivate a sense of admiration and reverence for Christ even in a general way is a very good place to begin with in the process of evangelism among Hindu *bhaktas*. For what else can be a better context to talk about God and Christ to a Hindu *bhakta* than the context of worship. Hence, if dialogue can serve initially as a preparation for evangelism among Hindu *bhaktas* then it needs to be taken into serious consideration for possible evangelism among them in the future.[266]

The main point is that any evangelistic attempt has to be based on personal experience. Any communication of the gospel to Hindu *bhaktas* will be effective only if it involves one's personal experience with Christ. Since this is predominantly experience- based, there is the obvious danger of one experiential account becoming unscriptural. Thus, it is paramount that a Christian's spiritual experiences be subject to the established, verifiable Christ of history and His teachings. Also, when a Christian talks about his personal experience with Christ, a Hindu *bhakta* is able to connect with that only if he or she has the same need. If the testimony does not connect to the immediate need of the *bhakta*, then the communication is not effective. All dialogue and conversation should eventually lead to the core issues of sin and forgiveness in Jesus Christ.

SMALL GROUP EVANGELISM

Indians like small communities because it feels like extended Indian families. Enterans would be interested in small groups, especially if there are other Enterans in the small group. The church can intentionally start small groups based on ethnic background, not to promote segregation, but to fulfill the herd needs of Enterans. Once the community need of Enterans is satisfied and they are comfortable in a Christian gathering, they will be more open to visiting a church.

This approach would seem segregating for the Inderican, but, for Enterans, it is a great way to fulfill their social needs within Christian community. Temples fulfill this very need for Hindus. Evangelism is more likely to be effective in the context of family than individually.

EVENT EVANGELISM[267]

Special events and courses are likely to attract Indians. Particularly attractive would be sporting events, social justice events, and events celebrating Indian culture, as well as courses on parenting, addiction, and health. This planning of events must be done with care for a distinction should be made between Hindu culture and Indian culture. Unfortunately, the Indian church traditionally misunderstands Indian culture to be Hindu culture, thereby missing a great evangelistic opportunity. Thus the Indian church fails to celebrate Indian cultural events, thereby denying entry points for Hindu seekers. In addition, some Indian churches refuse to celebrate even Christian events like Christmas and Easter, thus bringing evangelistic opportunities to a minimum.

Parenting seminars, marriage seminars, and any program that encourages the togetherness of a family will be attractive to Indians. This includes any age-appropriate ministry for different members of the family like summer school for kids, youth meetings, and children's church. Even if a church does not have strong family-based programs, they can work with other parachurch organizations to have regular seminars so that Hindus from the community would be invited to the church. For example, Parivar International, a Chicago-based organization, is committed to building up strong marriages and families among Asian Indians through seminars, retreats, and conferences.[268]

FREEDOM MINISTRY

Enterans are less forthcoming about addictions, including both substance and sexual. Indians in such situations are more likely to seek American churches rather than Indian churches to protect family and cultural honor. (For this reason, not many Indian churches, if any, have this type of ministry). Thus, American churches that have such programs can influence people with those needs. Indian churches that do not have any freedom ministry of their own can team up with parachurch organizations that work among addicts. Indian churches can, though, work with parachurch organizations to counter these problems in their community.

For example, Life Challenge International is an organization that is focused on Indian and Asian families that are under the bondage of alcohol and drugs. In addition to addressing the addiction issues of Enterans (usually men), they are also involved in providing support to the wives and children of such families.[269]

METHODS FOR INTRODUCING JESUS TO INDERICANS

Indericans are in a pre-evangelistic stage since they grew up in a Christian culture compared to Enterans who grew up in a Hindu culture. George Barna gives the following four methods that he thinks would influence Xers:[270] cell groups, provided they are discussion-oriented, non-confrontational, and non-imposing; social welfare-ministry opportunities that utilize a soft sell; lifestyle evangelism strategy; and Socratic evangelism, a dialectic method that has been in vogue in past centuries but has fallen into disfavor in this century.

LIFE STYLE OR FRIENDSHIP EVANGELISM

Within two years after an unbeliever becomes a Christian, he or she unwittingly loses all non-Christian friends. The progression is logical. The new believer wants to be around his or her new Christian friends and so loses, slowly, all his or her former non-Christian friends. Thus, believers need to be intentional in befriending and spending time with non-Christians. This time and effort spent is worth the investment. "It is so important that we make investments in friendships – what I sometimes call paying relational rent – in order to gain the person's trust and respect, as well as to earn the right to talk to them about spiritual issues."[271]

This type of evangelism predominantly entails purposeful relationship building for the sake of the relationship. Once a true friendship is established, evangelistic invitations will naturally follow.

The distinguishing characteristic of this approach is that it is based on developing significant, credible relationships with nonbelievers. The foundation of this approach is that you build an authentic, non-manipulative relationship with a nonbeliever, reflect a lifestyle that is overtly but not offensively different from the norm, raise the curiosity of the nonbeliever through such idiosyncratic behavior and have the opportunity at the request of the nonbeliever to describe the reasons and motivations underlying your unique way of life.[272]

This kind of evangelism needs a common interest. For example, a pastor will find it difficult to develop a deep friendship with students. Thus, the best people to reach other people are those with common interests – students can reach students, and physicians can reach other physicians. Unfortunately, the church cannot assume that lifestyle evangelism will naturally take place. Instead, churches need to have seminars on evangelism so that people know how they can be effective lifestyle evangelists. This kind of evangelism should be given more credence than it is now. It should be talked about, discussed, and planned.

Opportunities can be made to contact three types of non-Christian people.[273] The first are people *known* by the church members. Intentional social events can be planned with the intention to mix selected members of the "religious ranks" with those of the "renegade ranks," activities like golfing events, holiday parties, events for children on the block, pie parties for new neighbors, and baptism receptions. Also helpful are everyday events that involve others: sharing a meal, watching a game, sporting activities, exercise time, babysitting and work exchanges, children's activities and meeting up during the workday with colleagues.

The second kind of people to contact are people one *used to know*. One can meet or contact old classmates or friends and wait for opportunities to witness. As a result of social sites, it is possible to connect with people one knows and used to know.

The third kind of people to contact are people one *would like to know*. This is done by establishing acquaintances and later friendships with frequent contacts at the gas station, restaurants, dry cleaners, grocery stores, and clothing shops, for example. Lifestyle evangelism in general works as a three-step procedure: establish a significant presence in the life of a non-Christian, proclaim the gospel verbally, and persuade the other person to accept Christ.[274]

SOCRATIC METHOD OF EVANGELISM
One of the characteristics of postmodern thinking is the rejection of absolute truth. Thus there is also rejection of institutions or books that claims absolute truth.

Most young people reject absolute truth. … more than four out of every five Americans under the age of 30 contend that there is no such thing as absolute moral truth .… Exhorting young people to accept Christ because the Bible tells them to do so is rejected as a ludicrous reason for such a choice.[275]

Young people reject the imposition of beliefs. They want to draw their own conclusions. Even though these conclusions may be the same ones that their elders drew, they want the satisfaction of arriving at those decisions on their own.

This is where the Socratic Method is effective. In this method, it is essential for the teacher to have complete knowledge of the subject. He or she then asks probing, directive questions that do not manipulate the student but help to clarify the truth that is sought by the student. Socrates would start the discussion and invite his student to give his opinion. Socrates would then lead the student by continued questioning of the logic of the student's position, never stating that the student was wrong, but simply identifying the fallacies in the argument and asking the student to explain how those fallacies could be accurate. Invariably, the student would, by himself, arrive at a logical conclusion. This kind of a conversation is essential in a context that accepts all opinions and detests one person's absolute viewpoint. The goal here is be patient enough to let the hearer come to a conclusion on his or her own. Spiritual friends are those that introduce spiritual topics and then allows the hearer to come to spiritual conclusions on his or her own.

One of the most important skills of spiritual friendship is learning to respond to questions with more questions, not answers, just as Jesus did so often. …Spiritual friends, wherever they go, are gentle and persistent agents working against…contrary forces, patiently helping people to keep "thinking about it."[276]

In light of the rejection of absolute truth and the acceptance of everyone's story, telling one's story is a great way of evangelism.

Storytelling is the most effective way to reach this generation, because busters won't argue with a person's story. In fact, it may be their only absolute: everyone's story is worth listening to and learning from. Here's what needs to be communicated: "God's story intersected with my story; now I can share it with you so that you can consider making it a part of your story."[277]

The value of the Socratic method is to let the gospel story intersect with the Inderican's story, all the while enabling the Inderican to go down the path of truth and discover it for himself or herself in the context of the hearer's own story. E. Stanley Jones' method of round table conferences, mentioned previously, is effective among Indericans, too.

SMALL GROUP EVANGELISM

There are several advantages of a small group in evangelism. It gives a chance for a non-Christian to see Christian fellowship and values lived out without coming to church, and it provides a non-threatening place where non-Christians can ask pressing questions. There should be no pressure from the group members to persuade a person to come to church. Slowly, as they see Christian love and fellowship in action and doctrine lived out, they will be attracted to the gospel. It is a place to "hang out" with friends and enjoy fellowship because "people don't just want to learn about spiritual disciplines and be told to practice them on their own; they want and need the chance to actually practice them together."[278]

In addition, small groups can be a place to identify and use various spiritual gifts – the gifts of leadership, hospitality, encouragement, teaching or prayer, and evangelism.[279] An ideal group is from five to thirteen individuals. Also, every group leader should know the purpose and mission of his or her small group and how long the group is going to meet. The specific time period will help some groups avoid suffering the agony of a prolonged death. The church thus needs to be organized in the creation of new groups.

New people tend to join new groups. Those who are new to church or community tend to seek out others who are new. It is very difficult for a new member to break into a small group that is five years old with lots of history. Thus, the church should continuously start new small groups for newcomers so that everyone can be part of the history of that small group.[280] The new groups can be based on the many subgroups that exist within the church - students, singles, couples, couples with small children, families, or women. The reason small groups should consist of "like people" is so that there will be free flowing conversation and they will have similar needs, which can be answered together.[281] Based on the community and the needs in it, several different groups can be started: marriage enrichment, recovery, parenting, special needs, and leader training.[282]

Small groups are especially effective among Indericans because they want community, and small groups are ideal places to invite them. George Barna contends that "congregational bodies in the future will be decentralized and increasingly focused rather than centralized and multidimensional.[283] He thinks that the primary reason the second coming of the church will be from large churches to the small gatherings is because of the increasing need for community. Small groups fulfill the basic need for community. Jesus' band of disciples fulfilled the need for community. Indeed, Jesus' modus operandi was to have spiritual session over food, so much that his opponents called his disciples "gluttons." "Social networking in a post Christian world will primarily happen where people eat together in homes of Christians in neighborhood communities where faith is shared. Eating has always played a central role in the Christian faith."[284]

Postmodern evangelism will occur in casual Christian communities in which seekers are included. They will be able to see natural conversation and fellowship among Christians, who discuss the reality of Christian life in today's world. Innocuous social networking of Christians and non-Christians around a monthly meal can be the starting point of evangelism.[285]

EXPERIENTIAL EVANGELISM

The move from modernism to postmodernism is reflected in the transition from the logical to the experiential. Indericans need to experience the spiritual. They need to have a sense of the holy other. As for the singing, rather than the fast paced music of Boomer worship, Xers prefer slower contemplative worship where a clear sense of the spiritual drives the experience. In addition, Hindus come from a religious background that has vivid symbolism. Thus, from a generational and religious standpoint, Indericans need stimulation of the senses. "Participation and experience are very important to people in emerging generations, in all areas of life. They prefer to learn through interactive and participatory experiences."[286]

Kimball mentions that times of silence, the offering, open sharing, prayer, and especially communion are all experiential acts of worship.[287] All aspects of the worship service should be used for the experience of worship instead of just the singing. The sacraments are highly symbolic and highly experiential. This is where worship and the use of the sacraments can be key in people's spirituality. The symbolic "doing" of religion instead of merely "hearing" an intelligent sermon is more effective in the spiritual experience of the Gen Xer.

As symbols that mediate the divine in a very earthly context, sacramentals are ideal "media" for the experience of GenX spirituality… Sacramentals fit the GenX religious imagination. They frequently show up in pop culture, as well as in everyday experience. Rooted in the experiences of individuals and groups, sacramentals become integral to GenX's irreverent spirituality.[288]

Community-oriented evangelism will be effective in this post-modern age. There is also an emphasis in the living out of the doctrines rather than merely preaching them. This is a return to evangelistic methods of the early church and in the first centuries after Jesus. The initial chapters of the book of Acts tell of the community-focused church that resulted out of the early apostolic preaching. The community method was also used by St. Patrick in the fifth century among the Irish. His work was more of a movement than an institution, with small provisional buildings of wood and mud, a movement featuring laity in ministry more than clergy. This movement…was more imaginative and less cerebral, closer to nature and its creatures, and emphasized the "immanence" and "providence" of the Triune God more than his "transcendence."[289]

This type of evangelism is focused more on the community than on the individual, more on the experience than on reason, more on the application of truth than on the fact of truth. In the postmodern setting, each person is encouraged to come to the answer to the questions on his or her own, while living in a community.

Indericans will also be able to experience the Christian faith, ironically, in ministry teams. While they are ministering to others, they will be ministered to. Thus, opportunities should be given to Indericans to sign up to serve in ministry teams even if they are not believers.

SERVING AND CAMPUS EVANGELISM

There is a large need for compassion and justice ministries in most cities in America. The mere act of serving unselfishly will impact those who minister. Involving non-Christians in serving will help them to understand true Christian fellowship and love. However, first Christians themselves need to learn how to serve. "The important thing is that we serve the way Jesus did – selflessly, with no strings attached. Naturally one hopes that people will be influenced to come to Christ, but serving should never be done in a way that manipulates or forces them to do so."[290]

Newcomers to a city, including immigrants, need plenty of help in initially setting up a living. Churches in cities where there is a continuous movement of people could provide resources to newcomers. The options for service ministries are varied and many. Indericans can get involved in service methods like grief support ministry, food pantry, and ministry to the homeless, among others. Many times, those who will be impacted are those who do the service.

There are many Indericans and even Enterans who are students and stay in dorms. Indericans' desire for close-knit community in a campus setting can cause campus ministries to be effective. Many religious organizations recognize this, and so should the church. For example, International Students, Inc., is a student-centered organization that exists to see every international student befriended, led to a personal relationship with Jesus Christ, and discipled for His service in cooperation with the local church.[291]

FREEDOM MINISTRY AND EVENT EVANGELISM

Indericans who struggle with addictive behaviors can benefit from freedom ministries. Life Challenge International also works among Inderican and Asian youth that are involved in alcohol and drugs, usually unbeknownst to their parents. They also have awareness and prevention through churches, schools, and community camps.[292]

Events can be organized for Indericans, including half-day seminars on relevant, practical topics. Sermon/seminar topics relevant to Indericans are money management, dating, marriage, career options, questions of the purpose of life, parenting, finding their talents, and dealing with pain. Other events are sports events and music events that will enable Indericans to have fellowship together.

WEB EVANGELISM AND SEEKER SENSITIVE EVANGELISM

The purpose in browsing the Internet is not only for information, but also increasingly for relationship. Most of the information that people get is from the Internet. Churches should keep their websites updated with resources based on the needs of the community. To directly impact the different subgroups of a community, a church website can have different pages for each subgroup with relevant information. The increase in web presence will result in more people visiting the church worship service. With the proliferation and widespread use of social websites, churches can utilize this avenue to connect with church members, maintain blogs, and create a network so that non-members are able to see what the church is doing.

This intentional service setup by the church provides an opportunity for those who are interested in the Christian faith to explore and find answers to their questions in a welcome ambiance where they can maintain their anonymity and make their decision whenever they are ready. Some things that turn seekers off are boring, irrelevant sermons, asking for money, unfriendly church members, or bad nurseries.[293]

CONCLUSION

There are many methods available to have the Jesus Conversation to both Enterans and Indericans. Some methods work for both groups, but some others work only for either group. Once a church knows who their target group is, they can adopt appropriate methods for evangelism.

No amount of planning can substitute for the genuine personal relationship that should exist between the evangelist and his or her Savior, and no amount of organization can substitute for the genuine love that should exist between the evangelist and the Enteran or Inderican. All strategies and methods should flow out of these two relationships.

Notes:

264 Miller, *How to Build a Magnetic Church*, 17.

265 Alphonse, "The Gospel and Hindu '*Bhakti*,'" 280-288.

266 Alphonse, "The Gospel and Hindu '*Bhakti*,'" 290.

267 Peace, "Re-inventing Evangelism."

268 Sam George, Founder and Executive Director, email, April 22, 2010.

269 Binush Mathew John, Founder and Executive Director, Life Challenge International, email, May 1, 2010.

270 George Barna, *Evangelism That Works* (Ventura, CA: Regal Books, 1995), 112.

271 Bill Hybels, *Becoming a Contagious Christian* (Grand Rapids, MI: Zondervan, 1994), 98.

272 Barna, *Evangelism That Works*, 78.

273 Hybels, *Becoming a Contagious Christian*, 108-117.

274 Joe Aldrich in Barna, *Evangelism That Works*, 78.

275 Barna, *Evangelism That Works*, 108.

276 Brian D. McLaren, *More Ready Than You Realize* (Grand Rapids, MI: Zondervan, 2002), 48-49.

277 Zander, "The Gospel for Generation X."

278 McLaren, *More Ready Than You Realize*, 84.

279 Richard Peace, *Small Group Evangelism* (Downer's Grove, IL: InterVarsity Press, 1985), 27.

280 Callahan and Tanner, *Twelve Keys*, 36-37.

281 Callahan and Tanner, *Twelve Keys*, 68.

282 Peace, "Re-inventing Evangelism."

283 George Barna, *The Second Coming of the Church* (Nashville, TN: Word Pub, 1998), 178.

284 Robert E. Webber, *Ancient Future Evangelism* (Grand Rapids, MI: Baker Books, 2003), 58.

285 Webber, *Ancient Future Evangelism*, 59.

286 Dan Kimball, *The Emerging Church* (Grand Rapids, MI: Zondervan, 2003), 155.

287 Kimball, *The Emerging Church*, 159-169.

288 Beaudoin, *Virtual Faith*, 76-77.

289 George Hunter, *The Celtic Way of Evangelism* (Nashville, TN: Abingdon Press, 2000), 16.

290 Mark Mittelberg, *Building a Contagious Church* (Grand Rapids, MI: Zondervan, 2000), 322.

291 Sabu Joseph, Campus Staff, ISI, email, May 7, 2010.

292 John, email.

293 Peace, "Re-inventing Evangelism."

Conclusion

Most Enterans initially came to the shores of America in hopes of becoming financially secure and with the intention of returning to the home of their ancestors. They never conceived of settling down permanently in a foreign land. Many Indians who settled in other places like African countries and the Middle East eventually returned home. It is with that attitude that Enterans arrived in America. However, America, compared to most other countries, was made up almost completely of immigrants. Thus, welcoming immigrants was a part of American culture. Indians were thus welcomed and, as time went along, they realized that they could call this country home, too. Most Enterans considered America a foreign land when they arrived – it was Christian, Caucasian, and morally liberal. When they realized that they could be themselves without compromising their beliefs, they slowly began to accept America as their home.

Having children in America put at rest any doubts. Unlike some countries in the Middle East, where foreigners could never become citizens, Enterans could become naturalized citizens. Indericans, by virtue of having been born in America, automatically became American citizens. Indians became further rooted in America.

However, it is part of Indian-ness to never forget Indian culture. Thus, unlike immigrants from many European countries, Indians maintained their separateness, even as they attempted to merge into American culture. The welcoming arms of American culture had a place for the uniqueness of Indian culture and accepted its differences.

Hindus established places of worship and were given the freedom to continue their beliefs unhindered. However, Hinduism needed to be modified in order to survive in a non-Hindu context. In many ways, Hinduism is like American culture – it is able to accept all views, including opposing ones, and make them part of its own.

Enterans' perseverance to propagate Hindu Indian culture to their children enabled Indericans to develop a sense of connection with both India and Hinduism. However, since the context in which they were growing up is a non-Indian, non-Hindu context, it was inevitable in the long run that they would be influenced by the context.

The Enterans and Indericans can be mistaken one for another. Eventually, the conversations, attire, accent, and mannerisms can seem similar enough to confuse non-Indians. Many times, the difference can be seen only by other Indians. However, Enterans and Indericans are completely different groups of people. Enterans were raised in a predominantly Indian Hindu culture, are modern, older, and part of the Boomer generation; Indericans were raised in a predominantly American, Christian culture, are postmodern, younger, and Generation X. American churches who do not recognize the difference and Indian churches who refuse to recognize the difference will quickly find themselves unable to minister to either group. Indian churches will alienate Indericans, and American churches will alienate Enterans. Both groups require different strategies and different sets of methods.

In general, due to the innate desire of Enterans to experience Indian community, language, and culture, the best churches to reach Enterans are Indian churches that have services in specific Indian languages. Indian churches should, therefore, be started in every Indian language that is predominant in an area. Also, because of the revival in *Bhakti* Hinduism, Hindus are closer to the gospel of Christ than ever before. These churches should then focus their attention on trying to reach the Enteran generation, based on the predominant Indian language used in the church. Even though it is tempting for Indian churches to keep both Enterans and Indericans in the same service for the purposes of building Indian community, the needs of each are different, including their needs for community. Enterans want Indian community while Indericans want eclectic community. Indian churches, for the sake of their children, should be willing to let them go to an American church where they can grow spiritually. What they cannot do is to have a combined ministry that attempts to reach both Enterans and Indericans in one service/ministry. Unfortunately, since Enteran parents and Indian churches do not realize the uniqueness of Inderican culture and because of their need for Indian-ness, they often sacrifice Inderican spirituality on the altar of Indian culture. If an Indian church has the resources, it should begin a full-fledged separate ministry for Indericans without interference from Enterans. Also, a locality or a group of Indian churches can form one ministry for Indericans, where they can bring their non-Indian friends and experience the kind of community that they need. However, if Indian churches do not have such resources, then Indians should let their children go in order to experience a spiritual Christian life. Indian churches that attempt to minister to both Enterans and Indericans in one ministry will hurt the Inderican at the expense of the Enteran.

Due to the postmodern, Americanized, Generation X nature of the Inderican, they will be best reached by American churches or by Indian churches that have a specific separate service and ministry for them. If both Indian churches and American churches focused on the groups that they are naturally equipped to minister to, there would be an exponential growth of Indian Christians. The third generation and subsequent generations of Indian immigrants will be more American in their outlook and can be reached by American churches. However, the Enteran and Inderican in America are uniquely placed and need specialized methods of evangelism. Failure of an urgent, organized attempt to have the Jesus Conversation with Indians will result in the loss of Enterans to age and Indericans to the world.

Selected Bibliography

INDIAN CULTURE AND HINDUISM

Abraham, Kondoor. *The Asian Indian in the United States*. Pompano Beach, FL: Desh Videsh Publishing, 2003.

Agarwal, Priya. *Passage from India: Post 1965 Indian Immigrants and Their Children*. Palos Verdes, CA: Yuvati Publications, 1991.

Alphonse, Martin Paul. "The Gospel and Hindu '*Bhakti*': Indian Christian Responses from 1900 to 1985 – A Study in Contextual Communication." PhD diss., Fuller Theological Seminary, School of World Mission, 1990.

Akhilananda, Swami. *Hindu View of Christ*. New York: Philosophical Library, 1949.

Bauman, Chad, and Jennifer Saunders. "Out of India: Immigrant Hindus and South Asian Hinduism in the United States," College of Liberal Arts & Sciences, Faculty Scholarship, Butler University, 2009.

Dasgupta, Sathi S. *On the Trail of an Uncertain Dream: Indian Immigrant Experience in America*. New York: AMS Press, 1989.

Elliot, Michael. "India Awakens," *Time Magazine*, June 18, 2006, 38.

Fenton, John Y. *Religions of Asia*. New York: St. Martin's Press, 1983.

_____. *Transplanting Religious Traditions: Asian Indians in America*. New York: Praeger, 1988.

Gelatt, Julia, and Deborah Meyers. "Legal Immigration to the United States Increased Substantially in FY 2005." Migration Policy Institute. October 2006. No. 13 "Immigration Facts" http://www.migrationpolicy.org/pubs/FS13_immigration _US_2006.pdf (accessed April 13, 2007).

George, Sam. *Understanding the Coconut Generation: Ministry to the Americanized Asian Indians*. Niles, IL: Mall Publishing Co., 2006.

Helweg, Arthur W., and Usha M. Helweg. *An Immigrant Success Story: East Indians in America*. Philadelphia: University of Pennsylvania Press, 1990.

Immigration Act of 1965, Public Law 89-236, *U.S. Statutes at Large* (1965).

Indian Embassy, http://www.indianembassy.org/ind_us/census_2000/ia_population_map_2001.pdf (accessed May 7, 2010).

Jones, E Stanley. *The Christ of the Indian Road*. New York: Abingdon, 1925.

Kulandran, Sabapathy. *Grace: A Comparative Study of the Doctrine in Christianity and Hinduism*. London: Lutterworth Press, 1964.

Kurien, Prema A. *Kaleidoscopic Ethnicity: International Migration and the Reconstruction of Community Identities in India*. New Brunswick, NJ: Rutgers University Press, 2002.

_____. "Multiculturalsm and 'American' Religion: The Case of Hindu Indian Americans." *Social Forces* 85, no. 2 (December 2006), Research Library Core.

Larson, Gerald James. "Hinduism in India and in America." In Jacob Neusner, ed. *World Religions in America,* 4th ed. Louisville, KY: Westminster/John Knox Press, 2009.

Machado, Felix. "How Do Hindus View Jesus Christ?" *The Examiner,* October 10, 1998. http://www.hvk.org/articles/1098/0053.html (accessed December 7, 2009).

Mann, Gurinder Singh, Paul Numrich, and Raymond Williams. *Buddhists, Hindus and Sikhs in America: A Short History.* New York: Oxford University Press, 2008.

McKain, David W., ed. *Christianity: Some Non-Christian Appraisals.* New York: McGraw-Hill Book Company, 1964.

Morinis, E. Alan. *Pilgrimage in the Hindu Tradition.* New Delhi: Oxford University Press, 1984.

Neusner, Jacob, ed., *World Religions in America.* 4th ed. Louisville: Westminster John Knox Press, 2009.

Prabhupada, A.C. Bhaktivedanta Swami. *Bhagvad Gita.* http://www.asitis.com (accessed June 8, 2010).

Rudrappa, Sharmila. *Ethnic Routes to Becoming American: Indian Immigrants and the Cultures of Citizenship.* New Brunswick, NJ: Rutgers University Press, 2004.

Sikhnet, "Popular Indian Superstitions." http://www.sikhnet.com/sikhnet/discussion.nsf /By+Topic/9D4727920CFE8F7987256A340050CF72!OpenDocument (accessed March 2, 2008).

Sivananda, Swami. *The Divine Life Society.* http://www.dlshq.org/glossary.htm (accessed May 8, 2010).

Sudhakar, Paul. "How to Prepare the Church for Dialogue." *Religion and Society* 26, no. 1 (1979): 36-41.

Thorp, W. H. "Indigenous Christianity." *Harvest Field* 14, no. 11 (1912).

Warner, R. Stephen, and Judith G. Wittner, eds. *Gatherings in Diaspora: Religious Communities and the New Immigration.* Philadelphia: Temple University Press, 1998.

Wikipedia, "Non-resident Indian and Person of Indian Origin." http://en.wikipedia.org/wiki/Non-resident_Indian_and_Person_of_Indian_Origin#Indians_in_the_U.S. (accessed March 1, 2008).

Williams, Raymond Brady. *A Sacred Thread: Modern Transmission of Hindu Traditions in India and Abroad.* New York: Columbia University Press, 1992.

_____. *Religions of Immigrants from India and Pakistan: New Threads in the American Tapestry.* Cambridge: Cambridge University Press, 1988.

US Census Bureau, American Factfinder, United States General Demographic Characteristics: 2005, "Race," http://factfinder.census.gov/servlet/ADPTable?_bm=y&-geo_id=01000US&-ds_name=ACS_2005_EST_G00_&-_lang=en&-_caller=geoselect&-format= (accessed April 13, 2007).

US Census Bureau, US Summary: 2000, Table DP-1, http://www.census.gov/prod/2002pubs /c2kprof00-us.pdf (accessed January 19, 2008).

Zacharias, Ravi. "Reaching the 'Happy-Thinking Pagan,'" in *Growing Your Church through Evangelism and Outreach*, 1st ed., Library of Christian leadership, ed. Marshall Shelley (Nashville, TN: Random House, Inc., 1996).

EVANGELISM

Anderson, Leith. *Leadership that Works.* Minneapolis, MN: Bethany House Pub.,1999.

_____. "Leading and Managing Your Ministry." Lecture, Fuller Theological Seminary, January 31- February 4, 2005.

Arn, Charles. *How to Start a New Service.* Grand Rapids, MI: Baker Books, 1997.

Barna, George. *Evangelism That Works.* Ventura, CA: Regal Books, 1995.

_____. *The Second Coming of the Church.* Nashville, TN: Word Pub, 1998.

Beaudoin, Tom. *Virtual Faith.* San Francisco, CA: Jossey-Bass Inc., 2000.

Bosch, David. *Transforming Mission: Paradigm Shifts in Theology of Mission.* Maryknoll, NY: Orbis, 1991.

Callahan, Kennon L., and Ian B. Tanner. *Twelve Keys to an Effective Church.* San Francisco, CA: Jossey-Bass, 1997.

Goleman, Daniel. *Primal Leadership.* Boston, MA: Harvard Business School Press, 2004.

Green, Michael. *Evangelism in the Early Church.* Grand Rapids, MI: Eerdmans Publishing Company, 1970.

Grenz, Stanley J. *A Primer on Postmodernism.* Grand Rapids, MI: Eerdmans Publishing Co., 1996.

Guder, Darrell L., ed. *Missional Church.* Grand Rapids, MI: Eerdmans Publishing Co., 1998.

Hunter, George. *The Celtic Way of Evangelism*. Nashville, TN: Abingdon Press, 2000.

Hybels, Bill. *Becoming a Contagious Christian*. Grand Rapids, MI: Zondervan, 1994.

Jencks, Charles. "The Postmodern Agenda." In *The Postmodern Reader*. Edited by Charles Jencks. New York: St. Martin's Press, 1992.

Jones, E. Stanley. *Conversion*. Nashville, TN: Abingdon Press, 1959.

Kallenberg, Brad J. *Live to Tell: Evangelism in a Postmodern World*. Grand Rapids, MI: Brazos Press, 2002.

Kimball, Dan. *The Emerging Church*. Grand Rapids, MI: Zondervan, 2003.

McLaren, Brian D. *More Ready Than You Realize*. Grand Rapids, MI: Zondervan, 2002.

Miller, Herb. *How to Build a Magnetic Church*. Nashville, TN: Abingdon Press, 1987.

Mittelberg, Mark. *Building a Contagious Church*. Grand Rapids, MI: Zondervan, 2000.

Peace, Richard V. *Conversion in the New Testament, Paul and the Twelve*. Grand Rapids, MI: Eerdmans Publishing Co., 1999.

_____. "Re-inventing Evangelism." Lecture, School of Theology, Fuller Theological Seminary, Pasadena, CA, April 11-22, 2005.

_____. *Small Group Evangelism*. Downers Grove, IL: InterVarsity Press, 1985.

Randall, Robert L. *What People Expect from Church.* Nashville, TN: Abingdon Press, 1992.

Schaller, Lyle. *44 Ways to Increase Your Church Attendance.* Nashville, TN: Abingdon Press, 1988.

Schwarz, Christian A. *Natural Church Development: A Guide to Eight Essential Qualities of Healthy Churches.* Saint Charles, IL: Churchsmart Resources, 1996.

Shelley, Marshall, ed. *Growing Your Church through Evangelism and Outreach.* Nashville, TN: Random House, Inc., 1996.

Stanford, Eric. "The New Wave of Gen X Churches: Get Your Glimpse of the Future Here." *Next Wave.* http://www.next-wave.org/dec99/new_wave_ of_gen _x_churches.htm (accessed May 6, 2010).

Takle, J. "How Should We Missionaries Present Christ?" *Harvest Field* 12 (1901).

Thirumalai, Madasamy. *Sharing Your Faith with a Hindu.* Minneapolis, MN: Bethany House, 2002.

Walsh, Pakenham. "The Attitude of the Educated Hindu Mind toward Christianity," *Harvest Field* 17 (1906).

Warren, Rick. *The Purpose Driven Church.* Grand Rapids, MI: Zondervan, 1995.

Webber, Robert E. *Ancient Future Evangelism.* Grand Rapids, MI: Baker Books, 2003.

_____. *The Younger Evangelicals.* Grand Rapids, MI: Baker Books, 2002

Zacharias, Ravi. "Reaching the 'Happy-Thinking Pagan.'" In *Growing Your Church through Evangelism and Outreach*, 1st ed. Library of Christian leadership. Edited by Marshall Shelley. Nashville, TN: Random House, Inc., 1996.

Zander, Dieter. "The Gospel for Generation X." In Marshall Shelley, ed. *Growing Your Church through Evangelism and Outreach*. Nashville, TN: Random House, Inc., 1996.

Author Biography

Anush John was born and raised in the cosmopolitan city of Bangalore, India. The second of three boys, he was born into a pastor's home and grew up in a household devoted to ministry. At age 10, he gave his first sermon, and from that point he continued to pursue opportunities to teach and study the Bible.

Anush went to dental school in Bangalore, then partnered in a dental office until he married and moved to the US in 2003. During these years he also interned at Christian Medical College and Hospital in Vellore, which shaped his future professional interests and obtained a Masters in Divinity from Asian Institute of Theology, which refined his spiritual interests.

Post relocation to the United States, Anush went on to dental school at Boston, Massachusetts and medical school in Kansas City, Missouri and pursued a career in Oral and Maxillofacial surgery. He also concurrently worked on and completed a Doctor of Ministry degree from Fuller Theological Seminary, California focusing on Leadership and Evangelism. During medical school and residency he had the privilege of attending and being part of the teaching team at Liberty Christian Fellowship located in the Kansas City area. These years challenged, stretched, and enforced his passion for preaching and using his spiritual gifting.

He is currently in private practice in the Maryland region where he resides with his wife, Grace, and three children. He enjoys taking photographs, exploring various ethnic cuisines and attempting to learn French in his spare time.

www.ingramcontent.com/pod-product-compliance
Lightning Source LLC
Chambersburg PA
CBHW031338040426
42443CB00006B/385